A girl named Harlot

Kelly Kathleen

To the voices on the outside,

that sometimes became

voices on the inside

Hazel

1645. Think, sepia.

The Vermilliongate family had been gypsies for as long as they could remember, although they would never refer to themselves as Gypsies. We all know what they say about the Gypsies. The word Gypsy is the name given to travelling people or families living off itinerant trades, fortune tellers, people from Romani, wanderers, nomadic and the free-spirited — the meaning the town-people have given the word has a different connotation than traveller, fortune teller, wanderer nomad or free spirit. The town-people would say that gypsies are evil, that they practice witchcraft, weird rituals and dance with demons on stormy nights causing the wind to blow so hard it breaks the veil between this world and the next, opening the depths of hell.

The town-people didn't like, trust or speak to the gypsies. They feared them, and so, due to their terror, the gypsies were ridiculed, taunted and degraded.

The gypsy women were especially terrifying to the townies. They gossiped about the Gypsy women between each other telling stories of 'first-hand' accounts that they'd heard from so and so about one time when what's his face stumbled upon the 'truth' of what the travellers would get up to in the privacy of the trees, a few decades ago in the little woods.

They say, truth is belief accepted as fact, and to the towns people, this is what the obscene and ludicrous tales are - *their* version of truth. Case closed.

They held onto false tales as fact and forbade every town citizen young or old to ever speak to, acknowledge, look at or be in the same vicinity as an evil Gypsy.

The Townies were the most suspicious of Hazel.

Hazel is an extremely beautiful girl, the kind of beauty one would remember years later, even if only catching a brief glimpse of her.

Her most noticeable feature were her intense bright blue eyes, with tiny yellow flicks surrounding her pupil, her iris a light baby blue with a dark navy-blue ring giving her eyes an outline. They were so very blue and yet sometimes they could appear intensely green, depending on her mood. To be near Hazel meant her eyes were the focus - whether you wanted to or not. It was as if her eyes are glowing in the dark all the time.

Her bright baby-blues looking through to the very soul, as if they had the power to sense the heart's strongest desires and the spirit's truest purpose.

Something about her eyes made you want to trust her, like you could tell her your life story.. as if, perhaps, she already knew it…

Secrets never said out loud before, things buried deep and kept secret for a very long time.

This made the Townies extremely uncomfortable. If they dare make eye contact with her, confessions and unflattering confidential skeletons would pour from their mouths like running faucets.

Hazels skin was white as snow, soft and pretty like a lily, perfect like porcelain. She was so pale she had a similar effect of a yellow highlighter. To put it simply, she stood out. Where she went, heads turned. Everything about Hazel just seemed to *glow*.

Her hair thick and golden, face gentle and sweet —shaped like a heart. She's the most perfect portrait you've ever seen; a living, breathing porcelain doll, mesmerising people, glowing from head to toe. So.. it's pretty safe to say, women despised her. They turned green with envy at the sight of her, perceiving Hazel as a threat. They sought to destroy her, or, at the very least, taint her reputation so the men would think she was insane, too broken and too…*much*. Keep them away from her and next to them.

***

Last time Hazel entered a town was complete utter chaos, but that's a story for another day.

Hazel doesn't go into the towns anymore. Her family rarely would either. Once a week the Milk-man would come to find the family, wherever they may be. He delivered their mail, freshly baked bread and a large brown bag of potatoes. He never brought any milk with him, not once. Even so, nobody questioned why he was called 'the Milk-man', or how he found the family without failure each week.

What made the Milk-man an especially strange case was that he arrived at 11:11 every week on a Wednesday. No matter what the elements had in store, rain, hail or shine. No matter the date. Week in and week out. For as long as Hazel could remember.

The Milk-man would chat and laugh with Hazel, she didn't affect him the way she did others. He too, was strikingly beautiful, with skin as pale as snow, his eyes powerfully green with little flicks of yellow close to his pupil, sometimes turning turquoise in different lighting.

Hazel would ponder the Milk-man's life from time to time, though she wouldn't dare ask her mother or father if they knew anything about him. People didn't like questions, especially from a 'young lady'. The consensus: one must simply accept their fate the way it is and a young lady certainly had no business contemplating, thinking outside the box or god forbid asking questions. People around these parts didn't like to think in different ways from the crowd.

No siry-bob.

It was much safer to blend in and follow.

To be a young lady was to look pretty and to be seen, not heard. Never heard.

Hazel couldn't help but wonder about things. She'd wonder how the Townies knew about – or had 'heard' about her and her family. The family stayed in areas for short periods of time.

If by chance, the Townies hadn't heard of the family, they still were never fond of Hazel. She tried her hardest to fit in, to not stand out and to avoid looking people directly in the eye. She longed to know what it felt like to fit in and have friends to talk to, play and be silly with, to celebrate the good times and have by her side during the bad.

At least she had her family. She had four brothers, and three sisters: Rodger, the eldest of the siblings, Greg, Abel (Hazel would later name her only son Abel too) and Kevin.

Kevin and Abel had a six-week age gap between them... I guess every family has their secrets, but after a while things become the 'norm' and we become used to things as they are, tiring of questioning. Her sisters were Margret (Abel's birth mother), Florence and Martha. Hazel was closest with Martha. Her parents, Mary and Jack had been together since their teenage years. Jack's real name was John, but no one called him that. Mary believed she was special, she'd been named after Virgin Mary after all so she took the belief her name entitled her to be much holier-than-thou.

***

The family had a team of 8 horses that pulled the living-cart and all their belongings from A to B. Emerald, Diamond, Phoenix, Kathy, Belle, Dolly, Blackie, Nelly, Prince and Queenie. In a time of great depression, no-one had very much, so when Jack was offered the opportunity to make some money for his family, he jumped at the chance. All the older siblings were already partnered up, all of whom decided to live on the road and work with the rest of the Vermilliongate family. Jack always said, family stick together; come hell or high water. No matter what, and that's the end of that.

The family worked hard digging the trenches for irrigation systems around the towns in the area. Hazels father, brothers and brothers-in-law did the work— with the help of Belle and Nelly, who steered the work-wagon. Sometimes Belle would help dig channels the too.

The towns people did not like it one bit. Some of the more stubborn Townies refused to drink or use the water for 5 years after the systems were complete. All because the evil gypsies did it.

In a time of great depression, no-one had very much, so when Jack was offered the opportunity to make some money for his family, he jumped at the chance.

All the older siblings were already partnered up, all of whom decided to live on the road and work with the rest of the Vermilliongate family. Jack always said, family stick together; come hell or high water. No matter what, and that's the end of that.

All of the Vermilliongate's were home schooled, but from time to time, they were allowed to attend a 'Bush-School'. Tiny little institutions of education in the middle of nowhere, sometimes only 8 to 10 students attended a school, and that includes the Vermilliongate children.

When Hazel was younger and still attending school (she completed her schooling at eleven years old), there was one Principle that took great interest in her. He begged and pleaded with Jack asking him to allow Hazel to stay and complete her schooling, telling him how magnificently bright, talented and intelligent she was, and how, if nurtured and guided she would posses unlimited potential. The plea came to no avail. Jack simply would not hear of such an atrocity in his family unit. Hazel was a young lady and young ladies had no business with books or learning useless nonsense. Besides, the family must stick together. No matter what.

The Principle offered to have Hazel live with him and his family, there would be no expense to her, or the Vermilliongate family.

This too, fell upon deaf ears. Family sticks together and that is that. Jack had had two brothers die at a young age, one of pneumonia and one had drowned. This may be the reason why Jack was so adamantly unyielding on the family rule— although most gypsies were raised under the same tutelage. Aside from this, Hazel and her family were quite happy for the most part. They never argued, even though they never had much. At Christmas Hazel was pleased with a bottle of lemonade and a doll her mother had made out of old packaging. All the Vermilliongate's were very inventive and creative— you have to be when you don't have much. They found ways to meet all of their needs and created all necessities from old 'junk' and left overs.

Hazel was trying her hardest to study and study everything she could, to pull every last drop of wisdom from everything she encountered to unlock all her gifts, without actually knowing what she was doing, or whom she shared DNA with. In the back of her mind she knew she was gifted, and that she was something different. Hazel's downfall was she sometimes thought she knew better than others, as a Leo she was stubborn to the core, very impatient, a little bossy, outspoken and always looking for excitement. The spotlight following her where she go, unintentionally— she thought. All of which was okay, her heart was in the right spot. All she really wanted to be around people and help them. She had the heart and soul of a healer and gave more than she ever received in return. Her hands were conduits for a higher power and her eyes could *see* others. Her heart and stomach could feel the world around her with vast intensity sometimes too extreme to understand leading to anxiety and sleepless nights with unprecedented worry and concern her whole life through. She tried everything to quell her heavy heart, gut and restless mind from tonics and vitamin pills to essential oils and precious gems. None worked for her. Her mind was too powerful to conquer. She had the kind of instincts that lead to inner-knowings, Hazel could never accept what she knew, and she knew if she spoke out, she'd surely be condemned a witch. The universe makes no mistakes and we know what we need to know, when we need to know it. A task easier said than done. Her strong power required a lot of acceptance. She longed to know what it would feel like to be accepted.A dare to be different, unusual and unique, to stand out among the crowd and speak a truth fated to come riddled with opposition and ridicule. A task too heavy for Hazel to bear. She wanted so badly to fit in.

To be normal.

Still, she found herself wondering, what if?....

Hazel didn't sleep much, her mind would continue to throw different ideas around, a new way of thinking, and play out scenarios that would never happen.

Later in life, Hazel would become a nurse after marrying and for some time went off to do much needed work in another town— which, at the time, was unheard of. She always wanted to be a doctor (Hazel liked to be in charge) but, women were not doctors, doctoring is a man job…so she settled for as close as she could get — and she was a fine nurse.

Throughout her life, she never stopped her own learning and she carried a great love of reading, devouring books at a fast pace. The beauty of a book and knowledge never surpassing her.

***

Once a month, on the first Tuesday of every month, Hazels father, brothers, brothers in law and any other male around the site, would disappear for the entire night into the Little-Woods. This had happened for as long as Hazel could remember.

The men wouldn't return until the early hours of the next morning when the sun was beginning to rise. They gave no explanation where they were heading (nor did any of the women ask), what they were up to, who they might see or meet nor why it so ritualistically happened on the first Tuesday of every month, always leaving at 6pm on the dot. Once, Hazel had overheard her father say to a freshly-12-year-old Abel that they must leave at 6pm to be sure of a prompt arrival of 8pm, when their meeting would begin. She longed to know what they were doing and who they may meet in the Little-Woods. A very curious girl but of course she wasn't silly, and knew that no matter if she did work up the courage to ask—no one would tell a 'young lady' a damned thing. *It was against the rules.*

She had heard it time and time again; a young lady should not preoccupy herself with the matters of men. Ladies had more important concerns, like cooking, sewing, cleaning and, most importantly, finding a nice husband.

I really ought to follow them one evening.. but what if I were to be caught? What if I got lost?

What if I saw something I'd really rather not see, something there's no coming back from?.. And where was I supposed to tell Mother I was going? What would people think?

The too-curious-for-her-own-good, strange girl following the men around, sticking my nose in where it does not belong—-Hazel thought, deciding against the idea. It was much too risky.

Hence all the reading, keeping her nose in a book and out of other peoples business.

Well.. At least for the most part.

In Hazels mind, it was okay to read about what she pleased, any interest she could conjure up – and of course, she was interested in what the men were doing on their monthly meetings in the Little-Woods. Although, the books she found didn't give her the answers she longed for. Each book filled with more propaganda than the one before it. She couldn't help but feel there was something else at play here, something very odd happening right beneath her nose… And it concerned her that she was the only one curious with what was going on. Her truth pulling eyes were unable to gain anything of substance out of the men or the other women. Her power didn't work as well on her family. On days when they were a little tired it could work somewhat better, they'd laugh while answering Hazels questions—-she was very careful never to ask direct questions in fear of what might happen to her if she did. Sometimes they would slip up and make mistakes, but anything she tried to define later would be dismissed. They would insist they had never said such a thing and what a monstrosity it was for Hazel to enquire such nonsense. They told Hazel she was paranoid, loosing her marbles and thinking too deeply into things. Any slip would always turn out to be a 'joke' and they'd say she needed to lighten up on the conspiracy theories.

Hazel wondered if the Milk-man knew anything—or if he was involved. She had never thought to ask him. He seemed kind of....*different*, an outcast or a loner — just like her. She failed to imagine him joining any kind of group and she hadn't seen him converse with any of the men.

The Milk-man was an open fellow with Hazel and their conversations always rolled freely into extravagant topics, things Hazel couldn't discuss into such depth with anyone else. She very much loved when the Milk-man came to the sites.

An open mind is incredibly rare to cross paths with around these parts. Hazel loved lively conversations, the Milk-man enjoyed reading books too; no-one else she knew liked to read and they'd swap verses, ideas and stories from the pages they had skimmed the week before. Sometimes they'd even trade books and Hazel adored it. To her, there was no greater gift than a book. The gift of knowledge. The gift of feeling.

To Hazel it said, I want you to read what I've read, to feel what I've felt, learn what I've learnt and to experience what I have experienced.

A beautiful and touching gesture. She treasured those who exchanged or gave her some kind of written material. Curiosity was getting the best of her and so the next time the Milk-man came to deliver goodies, she would try to pry an answer out of him. She felt that at the very least, he would be honest with her.

As she made this decision, she realised how mysterious the Milk-man was. It hit her that, she did not know his real name, not his first name, a nick name, or anything besides 'the Milk-man'. It baffled her that after all their wild mercurial exchanges something as simple as a first name had escaped her. Maybe she ought to stop being so single pointedly focused on gaining knowledge and information, and instead interest herself with the personal attributes of those she came into contact with. She hoped the Milk-man hadn't marked her as conceded. She felt a little clueless, they say looking too closely will leave you missing the bigger picture, Hazel pondered what else she wasn't seeing.

Next time the Milk-man arrived she would ask for his first middle and last name, just to be sure —and to make up for it. She'd question him and find out his unique quirks, his life story, what made him tick —and she would actually *listen* to what he had to say. Hazel would have to wait until Wednesday to speak with the Milk-man.

Until then, Hazel would need a little entertainment. She was feeling bored and antsy lately and she hated it. It was a very annoying icky feeling when her spirit wanted to move, her feet were getting itchy —perhaps this was something normal for travellers to experience. She wanted to be free, out on the road, in the open and to stop feeling judged by those around her. Hazel knew she was nearing some kind of important milestone but she was yet to figure out what it could be. There was a cross road ahead of her, and she often wondered about her true passions and her life mission. She'd wonder where it was all heading, feeling lost and unsure of the *right* answer.

When she did get a wink of sleep her dreams were vivid and colourful.

She worried about their meanings, and questioned sharing them with others, concluding they'd think she was mad.

All she dreamt was most impossible, filled with symbolism of extraordinary lunacy.

The hardest part of putting meanings to symbols is that it has to be true for the *individual*. What is true for one, may not be true for the next; and that is the beauty, and the curse of a symbol. Countless meanings each as unique as a snowflake or fingerprint. Hauntingly beautiful indeed, yet confusing when one is unsure what to think and can't trust themselves. It's like being too close to a puzzle and struggling to find the correct piece, when it has been right in front of you all along. Sometimes one does not think so clearly when it comes to the self, we fumble, draw a blank and over-analyse.

The universe must just laugh at some of the obvious coincidences and messages that are ignored or not seen.

Hazel would freeze each and every time she even thought about letting her dream-world out into the real-world, to another person. She had the idea to perhaps speak with the horses about her dreams first to help her grow the confidence to confide in a human being. Each time she tried to articulate the words, no sound left her mouth. She told herself, even Queenie and Diamond would think she'd gone mad, insane, totally bonkers, a complete loony. She held the notion that someone may eavesdrop or see her conversing with horses and she would wind up in the nut-house. This time, fear had defeated her.

It was time for the family to move on. The pendulum had swung, and landed on a small town called: Confinedville.

Hazel's thoughts had been consumed by the Milk-Man, what questions she could ask him, her very strange dreams and where all the men wander off to on those peculiar Tuesdays. She was distant and lived in her mind, until she heard of the families plan to finally move on. There was something about Confinedville. She wasn't sure what was in store for her yet but she was felt drawn to this place, like it was 'meant to be', as if her fate and destiny were drawing closer....that is, if destiny really did exist....

***

The Vermilliongate family had lots to pack for people who didn't own much. They decided to leave the day after tomorrow. It was the middle of summer and man, was it hot. Greg and Billy (Martha's Husband) had been trying to make Jelly in the clay keeper for the past three weeks, but during this heat wave, no such luck. They'd checked it this morning, the jelly still wasn't set. Just before the family left, they ended up drinking it.

Tonight the Vermilliongate's, and a few other families would sit for a feast. There was no way of knowing if the other families would cross paths ever again —which goes hand in hand in a travellers lifestyle.

Good-byes could last a life time, so, when ever the family was ready to leave for their next venture, a celebration was in store. The mood always high and light-hearted, the night forever a positive memory to treasure. Hazels father Jack would tell her, "Goodbyes are nothing to be frightened by, you oughtn't feel nostalgic when you leave people behind, the road is long, our encounters with another are always what they are supposed to be...The man upstairs makes no mistakes. Paths truly meant to be together are so strongly intertwined, like an impenetrable ball of twine, not even the Devil herself could separate with the help of a thousand fallen angels. So bless those we wave goodbye and thank them for each and every lesson they delivered while present, not worrying whether it felt good or bad. All being a teacher, may our learning never cease."

Another thing Jack always said which was of interest to Hazel was "I'll be seeing ya" every time he would part ways with someone. Hazel felt like her Dad was among one of the wisest men she would ever meet. His outlook stayed uncommon in a spiritually charged kind of way his whole life through.. or maybe he was just really high. Who knows, either way —Hazel enjoyed it and it amused her to listen to him rant.

The farewell feasts were always magnificent. The gypsy women knew how to throw a few ingredients together. They prided themselves on the ability to look after the family. The women were the care givers and everything in-between. A gender role fulfilled to a tee.

Hazel didn't want that role.

She wanted to be free and to follow where her heart may take her. While she loved helping, cooking and felt called to look after every living being around her, the classic wife role irritated her. She wanted to leave her mark on the world and affect more people than a husband and children.

Hazel sat beneath a big red-gum a short distance from the families camp site, allowing her imagination run wild. Day-dreaming infinite possibilities of what may lay ahead. She loved the company of nature, the birds, the bees, the flowers and the trees. Plenty of butterflies and dragonflies to stare at. Her love of animals outweighed the connection she had with people and all the critters and creepy crawlies she met seemed to love her too. Animals seemed to swarm Hazel, which was unsettling to most, a sense of jealousy rising when they witnessed her natural charm in the animal kingdom.

"Hazel?..HHAAZZZEEEELLLL!" her Mother called out to her while pacing the luscious long grass between the pair. "I've been calling out to you for yonks! We've got a feast to prepare! What on earth are you doing all the way out here wasting time day-dreaming. A young lady needn't waste so much time thinking, there are things to do, mouths to feed, folks to take care of!" Mary yelled, shooting a ball of frustration into Hazels dreams. "I apologise Mother, I was just thinking about.." Hazel spoke softly, trying not to enrage her mother more than necessary. "Never mind what you were thinking, get a move on, you're roasting the vegetables, we need extra potatoes and help setting the table..quickly! C'mon, chop-chop." Her mother ordered. The instructions were non-negotiable. Mary was not a woman to bicker with — unless you wanted a slap across the ear. Hazel stood quickly, and jogged over to the rest of the women to begin peeling potatoes. Her mother speed-walking behind her muttering to herself as she made her way back to the campfire oven "fancy, a young girl preoccupied with her intellect, her father should have never started her on those blasted books. God-damned novels, the only thing worth reading are the Lord's pages."

Hazel chose to ignore what her mother was saying to herself. Books were one thing she would not dismiss, no matter the disarray it caused to her mothers virtues and regulations of a ladies habits.

Hazels filled her minds eye with an array of prosperous visions, telling herself: 'How will anyone know if I keep my thinking to myself?'

***

When Hazel reached the campsite her father was poking the fire with a stick, all the horses surrounding him. Hazel admired her father's relationship with his team of horses.

After the working day, the horses were free to roam and do as they pleased. None of the horses ever attempted to run away, or strayed far. If by chance one of the horses did journey some distance to find a nice patch of grass to munch on, all it took was a mighty whistle from her father and all the horses would immediately gallop towards him. Jack was very particular about his horses. Of a morning, no-one would leave for work until the horses had at least an hour feeding time, the team fed before the family. Their breakfast was to be earned.

A collar was never put on any horses until they had all been thoroughly brushed and curry-combed. Jack never, not even once, got on the caravan or pulley when travelling from town to town, instead he walked along side his team of horses the entire way.

Hazel was peeling potatoes, trying to keep her mind from wondering, to be in the moment and please her Mother. To help her stay present, she started a conversation with her father. She loved his wisdom and unique knowledge, the type of knowledge gained only through life experience. He told daring tales of his past, present and sometimes he'd predict the future. Hazel pondered for a moment the right words to spark his interest. After a moment of quiet with only the sound of the fire crackling, Hazel broke the silence. "Father, why is it that you never ride our horses, nor the caravan or pulley? Why do you walk *with* them?" She said. Jack looked at Hazel then took his gaze to the sky's brilliant blue vastness with child-like optimism, a small twinkle in his eye. "Well, my girl, because I am one of them. A member of the team, a team I am so lucky to be apart of. I walk beside them to experience what they do, to feel what they feel and to see what they see, to see the world through the eyes of a gentle beast. A particularly magnificent creature. I do it to know simplicity and equality, so my horses know we are equal. I hope to lead by example. I walk beside my horses because, in all honesty, I don't feel deserving of being carried around by these wonderfully lovely souls. They are not here for me, or for you, or for any of us. They are here to please themselves and if they want to leave then I wish them well. Their eyes hold wisdom unknown to any man and I wish to know the strength they gracefully hold within"

And with that, Hazel had fallen into deep deep thought.

What is a horse's perspective?

She had not sat with an idea like it before.

Did horses love? ...Well, of course they must.... Did they love humans?

Hm, well perhaps a select few —they did seem to be very fond of father, and they weren't trying to run away. How do they communicate? Are they telepathic? Or perhaps they simply judge based on body language? Perhaps they have sixth sense and can feel energy...

Again, true to habit, she had fallen down a rabbit-hole in her mind, one thought always leading a long train to another, then another and so on.

To say the least, she was a day-dreamer, a free-thinker, an introvert seeking answers and wasting her time away in her mind.

Hazel compiled all these questions concluding she will never be able to, not in her life time, or in a million years, have a definite answer.

People and animals cannot communicate - not in the way she would like to, with words and direct answers. Maybe we will never fully comprehend one another; and perhaps, we're aren't supposed to.. She snapped back into reality, realising the time that had past while she was zoning out.

Again.

Idealising the life of a horse.

She looked up at her father, and he was off with the fairies.

Quietly she went back to the half peeled potatoes, quickly finishing the job before her mother came to check and witness her procrastination.

Her mother was not a fan of procrastination, of anything she deemed unproductive, often she would remark that Jack and Hazel could live multiple lifetimes solely on their wasted minutes in the lands of their minds.

Hazel would think to her self: *Well, we always get the jobs done, and for that matter, we are always finished our chores long before anyone else, so whats the big deal if we are thinkers, dreamers and storytellers. Who was her Mother to say that was not useful?*

Who knows, maybe one day it will even be renowned as a talent, a skill...maybe it already is and her Mother just can't see it, or she see's it and doesn't like it because she cannot do it...

At the feast, which had become a large get together, (although there was still too much food put out) Hazel sat quietly trying to fade into the background, observing her company for the evening.

People watching was one of her favourite past-times.

She felt it was an intriguing investigation, human behaviour was a fascination of hers and she could, or rather, *would* spend hours watching others with her eagle eye, contemplating what their actions could tell, why one had done this or that, or why they used this tone of voice instead or another. She tried to guess, and sense how each individual might feel, if what they were doing and saying actually fit what they were thinking on the inside.

She wondered what they could possibly be hiding or if their thoughts were written all across their face.

How does one decipher if action, thought and feeling are aligned within another?

She'd then go into what she felt in the moment and question if *her* emotions were controlling what she was thinking and feeling.. or if they had been passed on from someone else? What do we really know about emotion and what happens if one does not acknowledge a feeling within themselves? Where does it go?....

"Hazel!" her mother snapped from the end of the table, "can you pass the potatoes, pla-easee?" Hazel grabbed the bowl and passed it down the table. She looked down at the plate that had been filled for her and started shovelling mouthfuls in, trying to avoid conversation. She'd look down every time someone met her gaze, avoiding eye contact with everyone sitting at the long wooden table. Her mother had instructed her to act 'normal' around others. It was exiling enough being a travelling family, let alone a traveller that acted strangely, questioned the unseen mysteries of the world, communicated with animals and told fortunes. 'Must you be such a cliche', her mother would say. The rumours already flew around about the Vermilliongate family and her Mother didn't want people to have any more ammo at their disposal.

Hazel complied to her Mother's wishes and didn't talk of 'nonsense' around people outside the family but small talk wasn't her thing so she kept her mouth shut for the most part while others made ordinary, boring chit-chat.

She vaguely listened in to pieces of dialogue being exchanged person to person, taking note of what 'normal' is. She couldn't help but think how very pointless the whole scenario was; exerting precious energy vocalising language back and forth like a predetermined tennis match. She watched as no-one listened, politely waiting for their turn to speak, occasionally nodding, and pretending they were hearing every word.

Hazel was still obsessing about the Milk-man.

Her eagerness to see him becoming almost unbearable, taking up most of her waking hours. She had a few days to wait until the next encounter, before the family would arrive at their next destination and the Milk-man would find his way to them.

It was the day the family would bid their farewell to their latest home and voyage many roads to their brand new home. The saying 'all roads lead to home' rang true for the Vermilliongate's, it struck a different cord for those with travellers blood. The road *is* home. Once everyone was packed they'd hit the road again. A job easier said than done. First, tents and personal belongings must be packed, tidying any mess left around the area and then, the fun part; packing up the animals.

Hazel had her cats and took pot plants everywhere she went. The plants would often fall off the back of the cart during trips which irritated her Father. The family had chickens which had to be captured before leaving. The chooks were Hazel and Martha's responsibility. Which is probably why the girls were such good runners. Once, at a bush school, Hazel had to race herself at the school athletics day as there were no other children in her age group. All the other kids there cheered as she ran. She won. Martha went to 17 bush schools in total, which she felt made her well-learned. The family owned a cow. Betsy's her name. Betsy had taken some leave from the family a little while back, a couple of towns ago. The family and a few other travellers had a substantial amount of money stolen from them by a man promising many business opportunities, and, given the state of the economy at the time, it was great news…too good to be true. Their mother, Mary, had seen the man-of-promise put his light on during the middle of the night and pleaded with Jack to go check what was going on, Jack would not go. He said that no-one would rip off good folk, especially with families to feed.

Jack continually saw the best in all people, he truly believed all people were good.

In the morning, the man was long gone. A kind farmer whom lived near by had heard of what had happened and offered to buy betsy from the family, he would take care of her and she would be right here waiting for them when the family returned with enough money to purchase Betsy back again.

It only took two jobs to earn enough money to make their way back and reclaim their beloved cow. So, in the end, the good of people did prevail…*eventually.*

***

The family got on the road and Hazel was full of romanticised illusions of her new life and the answers she was sure were awaiting her, the new friends she'd make and of course, what would happen when she finally crossed paths with the Milk-man again. "Just a few days" her father said, when she asked how long it shall be until they arrive.

Hazel grew more impatient with every second that passed her.

She knew —she just *knew* something meant just for her was at this next destination.

The clip-clop of the horses feet played a kind of mediative tune for her. She began to draw to pass the time and to help quell her 'what could be' anxieties. Hazel felt art could really teach you so much about self, the way you really feel, emotions suppressed spilling out onto the blank page, hidden thoughts, messages and a connection with the soul. Today was not one of those days.

Creativity cannot be forced. There is no structure to imagination.

She tried and tried to get something, anything out onto the blank white page.

Clip, clop, clip, clop.

The pencil moved as she breathed in and out.

Inhale. Exhale.

As she calmed, it was as if the pencil guided itself, as if someone, something else was adding their own input to her artwork.

Before she knew it hours had passed and she had a magical realm of fairies coming to life on her page. A magnificent fairy kingdom. Her imagination pondered if they could, or ever resided somewhere, hidden from the view of humans.. No time for silly thoughts, it was time for tea, she must feed her animals, set up her tent and go to bed. Hazel prayed tomorrow was the day the family would finally arrive at their semi-permanent home. Luckily, she had a good book to preoccupy her and pass the time before she fell asleep. She came across an old favourite while sorting her clothes for the day ahead. Hazel had not yet outgrown fairytales, and she hoped never to do so, she thoroughly enjoyed a good fable filled with possibility, adventure, magic and overcoming the improbable with a little added romance. She didn't see why she would ever have to leave that part of herself behind.

The next day passed quickly with the help of the written word and the clip-clop of the horses in the background. Tomorrow the family would arrive at the outskirts of Confinedville. She fell asleep easily that night and slept peacefully for the first time in a long time. The following morning, they packed their tents and set sail. Jack leading the team. By nightfall their new beginning would close in and Hazel would no longer have to day-dream of what might be….

∗∗∗

****

Perspective switch

****

Harlot

Today. Thinking turns Colour.

Dear diary?…
I think that's how you're supposed to start these things.
Once upon a time?
My psychologist, Dr. Hodoyafel, said that getting it all down on paper would help. She believes I need to find a way to connect with people. Seems stupid to me, I'm happy to be alone —but I have to do it, so here I am. I do 'talk therapy' with her wherein she lectures me on the importance of good posture and gives me tips how to connect with others, then she reports what she 'finds' to a Psychiatrist. She diagnosed me with Schizophrenia two years ago and so now, with the help of the Psychiatrist (whose name I don't even know, every now and then she'll stand in the corner while Dr. Hodoyafel and I do talk therapy), I'm on antipsychotics like Haloperidol along with some others I cannot spell or pronounce. Dr. Hodoyafel told me she tried to keep me off drugs for as long as possible but nothing else worked. Anyway, here goes. *Where do I begin? Thoughts? Feelings? My story?*
Apparently I jumble words, and repeat myself, but I'll do my best to make sense. She thinks it might be easier for me to write than to speak.
I suppose I'll start with my name.
Harlot Vermilliongate.

So, the dictionary says that Harlot means prostitute, or a whore; basically someone who doesn't own their own body. I was named Harlot because my body was sold before my birth. I am a vessel for others to possess. It's not as exciting as it sounds, I never remember when it happens. They must have thought it was hilarious to name me Harlot, a little stab in the heart. I've actually grown quite fond of it now. It's unique. So, obviously, my life is... *strange*.

When my grandmother was a young girl, she didn't lead a normal life or have a normal up bringing. She didn't live in house, not until she married my grandfather at 19 years old. Her family didn't stay around one place for too long. She was, what some people call a gypsy or a traveller. My Grandmother told me that when she moved into a house she hated it. It made her feel boxed in, stuck in between walls, like a human cage. She had moved into my Grandfathers house with him once they had married. It was the house my great-great-great-great Grandfather passed down to him. The house my family and I live in now. The house has been passed down from son to son since 1852. It's a huge two story red brick house and it's always cold. The house has 21 rooms, an attic and a wine cellar that my great-great-great-great Grandfather added to the house when prohibition was in place and he needed somewhere to hide his alcohol..and somewhere to drink it.

Although, apart from that I don't really know too much about anyone in my family —not because I fail to enquire; I'm quite the inquisitive and curious type, but my family are private people, they're all kind of...*secretive,* and we never get too deep.

Why, they could be living double lives for all I know.

Ha!

I highly doubt that.

Nothing of any excitement ever happens around here.

My family is the founding family of some social-group-type-thingy that has been running for centuries but from what I can tell, all they do is gamble and use it as an excuse to drink a tonne on a Tuesday night. It's so boring I've even forgotten the name of it. I have four brothers and they are all apart of it.

We live in Confinedville, a small rural town by the river.

Pretty buildings and paddle-steamers, ripe in history yet small-mind syndrome consumes the people.

For the most part in Confinedville, people go to work, to jobs they despise, come home to partners they cannot stand, then, they drink away their sorrows, bottle after bottle. Perhaps a little drug abuse to numb the pain. Cocaine, MDMA, gear, weed, whatever you want, we've got it in Confinedville, no need to feel ashamed, everyone is on something here. My Father has abused substances since before I was born, so growing up under him was a lot of fun. There's a bit of meaningless drama for entertainment, which results in endless gossip about friends and colleagues to help pass time. I'm the weird kid, the odd ball, that strange girl, the black sheep, the loner; and I don't have my own money so apparently my vote doesn't count too much among the land of the living. Animals seem very fond of me, I draw them in easily. My best and only real friend is a loyal red-heeler, named Daisy I rescued from the pound, we go everywhere together and she stays by my side wherever we go.

My grandmother always tried harder than most to understand me.

A lot of my personality structure comes from her. I get my eyes from her too, bright baby blue with dark circles to line the outer iris; quite the blessing, huh?

Wrong.

Most people I meet tell me my eyes creep them out, they're weird and strange..*too unique.*

Being different from everyone else doesn't exactly entail big self esteem levels.

Growing up criticised, beaten up and beaten down, laughed at and incessantly ridiculed wormed it's way inside my mind as years rolled on...but, I guess, what would you do if your child was communicating with the dead?

Doing strange things like talking to the trees and insisting that fairies were coming around at night..? (As my father would say, 'that kid made me hit it'.)

That was then, I've outgrown queer-ness now. I don't believe anything that science doesn't back up...

My family dynamic has always been more than a little complicated.

From the outside, we look like the normal picture perfect family.

I recall kids at school saying to me they wish they had my family...What goes on behind closed doors, stays hidden in the walls.

Addiction runs in the family and addictions don't make for pleasant times, I remember a lady once telling me 'happy people don't do drugs' and I think she was right.

In fact, all of my relationships are complicated.

I have a few friends but I think when the relationship you have with yourself is rocky, so is everything else. I don't really know exactly who in the world I am, which makes it difficult for other people to connect with me.

It makes it hard to connect with myself. I don't know what I want.

I feel like an alien in a peculiar and lonely world that I do not belong in.

It has been that way since my first day on this earth, which was an extremely long and painful ordeal for my mother.

24 hours in labour and when I was dragged into this realm by the doctor, I was yellow and had a cone-head, looking like a real-life alien.

I don't believe in aliens.

A silly little conspiracy theory.

If science cant prove it, it's not really real to me.

Which is why I ignore the things I see.

It's not real..just apart of my imagination.

I learnt that long ago.

Just like Stevie Nicks, I keep my visions to myself.

I'd much rather not wind up in the loony bin.. like they all said I would.

When I was a little girl I believed in everything. I carted my vivid imagination everywhere with me, exercising it regularly.

I'd always have my nose in a fairytale, I'd be riding a broomstick, telling magnificent fables about magic and mystical creatures I'd come into contact with, or making little fairy gardens equiped with mushroom homes for the fairies to dwell in.

All of this, was encouraged by my Grandmother. She was in to stones and gems, forever wearing a gold-chain with a Celtic-cross pendant (that she would clutch at when she was thinking really hard.) She gifted me a square peridot ring at a young age, which she told me had 'special powers' and would compliment my Virgoan traits. I rarely take the ring off. I don't know about the whole special powers and all that jazz, science says crystals are simply placebos —but it's a nice ring.

I remember as a child, questioning the credentials of Santa Claus. I couldn't contain the hunch I had that he just wasn't real. The story didn't add up to me. I followed my mother around for days on end asking if he actually existed. Eventually she tired of it, and shouted "FINE! No! He's not real!"

The world of make believe died to me that day

I called my family a bunch of liars and gave them the silent treatment for a week.

After that belief dwindled, I remember a little while later, going to my Nanna's house and she suggested I make a fairy garden.

Reluctantly, I adhered.

I created a really nice little home, with a pink and purple castle and pretty colourful stones. I can remember as clear as day staring at the little fairy land I'd made and for a long time, telling myself

'I know they are there, fairies are real, where are they?

I know they are real, why cant I see them anymore?'

After that, I stopped wasting my time on childish beliefs and silly imagination…that was, until my Nan passed on. Watching somebody you love wither away in palliative care has the power to change a person to their core. The experience is bleak and confronting. It causes us to face that death is the reality, and one day, we will have to do it too.

While my Nan lay there with 'death rattles', I remember thinking *'No. Nan isn't dying. Nan's a fighter, she will get better'.*

She didn't.

It was her time to move on and her soul left her body.

Sometimes I feel, we, take each other for granted. It's only when our loved ones leave this world do we appreciate how much they meant to us or even realise what they did for us.

All the little things.

The food cooked with extra love, the care, attention and acceptance.

My Grandmother gave me my copy of *The Velveteen Rabbit*, an all time childhood favourite of mine, I have it sitting on my bookcase right now. She made clothes for me so I could showcase my differences —and so no one had the same stuff as me. Nanna was a Leo, which rules the heart. True to form Nan touched the heart of every person she encountered. Nan was a care-giver, she took care of us all and never asked for anything in return. She was warm, friendly and had an infectious laugh. She cooked, she cleaned, she bossed us around. I remember Nan spending entire days cooking so each Grandchild, and Pa, would have their favourite desert —then she'd just place the bowl in front of you and then walk off. Food was her love language, and none of us will ever forget her famous lemon cheesecake. She collected any and every keepsake/sentimental item her family had. For years she's been collecting the limited edition 50cent coins to pass on to her Grand-kids. She also had her fiery side, if you swore in front of her, you could expect a clip under the ear. When one of my cousins was a kid, he was peeing outside at the farm and a rooster began to attack him, so Nan comes from out of no where, bashes the rooster and cuts it head off, turns to my cousin and says "well, he wont do that again" —and walks off. My cousin said he never pissed in front of a rooster again, not unless Nan was there. We laughed about this story for about 20 minutes.When she passed I wrote her eulogy —with ease, words flow quickly when they come from the heart. I wasn't to read it out-loud myself, but the funeral officiant did a beautiful job with her gentle-toned, yet confident voice. I wear her Gold-Celtic-cross everyday. Grief changes everything about a person. Losing a loved one opens the mind to ideas one would not previously be open to. It's the power grief holds. I could feel my Nan around me. All the time. I doubted I held the ability to communicate with the dead and that it was all in my head. I convinced myself it was. As time went on, I'd see more and more images of something, or someone out the corner of my eye, but when I'd turn to look, they would disappear. Doubt is such a mighty foe and I couldn't just blindly believe what I was seeing and hearing It was at this point, I felt I was going insane. Feelings are not validated in the everyday so going on 'a hunch' isn't held as a medallion of sanity or seen as well-mental-health, even I knew that.

It was at this realisation that I had a strong urge to go for a walk —which was normal, I often take walks along a path by the river called Scenic drive (one of my favourite places in the world... although, to be fair, I haven't ventured far from Confinedville..only to the pages of a book.) which is surrounded by nature with plants, trees, bushes, birds, butterflies and dragonfly. The sunshine helps to clear my head and I've always felt fairies live there, again, another silly hunch, but this day was different, I was being pulled there by something. I was feeling particularly depressed, and I was giving up but off I set.

Only a short distance along, something told me to look up from the dirt road. A huge swarm of dragonfly flew directly above me, as high as the tall gum-trees.

The swarm followed me the for rest of the track, flying high above my head.

Before this day, I had never witnessed more than two or three dragonfly together. I read somewhere that you only see dragonfly if they *allow* you to see them, and that they zig-zag between this world and the next —and they are highly associated with the fairy kingdom. As I neared the end of the walking track, where the path becomes sandy and the gum tress fade to bushy shrubs, the dragonfly came closer, darting in circles surrounding my body. Amazed that this was even happening I reached to get my Iphone from my pocket hoping to capture the spectacular moment on camera, so I could prove it to others —and to myself.

I flicked the phone into video mode as quickly as I could and began recording, but when I watched the video back I couldn't see a thing due to the way the dragonfly move. Not one of them was visible to the screen. And then, just like that, they vanished into thin air. I guess its true, dragonfly are only seen if they choose to be…

I stood in the same spot, I looked down and at my feet lay a pastel pink and purple card. It was a business card that read:

Enchanted Thorns. Intuitive Readings.

There was a phone number underneath the titles. The back of the card had a little slogan *'for the beauty of a rose, first, we must water the thorns..'* Right away with my phone still in hand I called the phone number on the card, I had to, I mean, it was left by dragonflies. A lady answered the phone and said her name is Asta.

She sounded kind and warm. I didn't say anything to her about how I had found her information..and she didn't ask.

Little did I know —I had just opened pandoras box.

****

I woke the next morning butterflies fluttering in my belly.

I left early for the train. Asta lived in the city three hours away. I made small talk with the ticket-lady as she came to check my ticket. She had a little diamond stuck on her front left tooth. I always made a point to look people directly in the eye. I'd heard it was the looking glass to the soul and I believed you could tell a lot about a persons character, and their strength from the eyes. Aside from that, it's respectful.

I remember distinctly that as I made eye contact with this lady midway through her sentence she went blank and looked dazzled,. This had happened a lot and I wasn't sure why but, it never really stood out to me, until this day, then I could recall many experiences where total strangers would spill their entire life story to me upon meeting me only moments before, including intimate and personal details, things they said they had never told anyone or said out loud before. I had grown used to it and normalised it in my thoughts.. *until now.*

"What is it?" I said to the ticket-lady with the diamond on her tooth, my tone soft, slightly smiling to ease the fear she appeared to be feeling.

"Umm, ahh, nothing dear. I've got to finish checking the rest of the tickets" she said before hurrying away to the next carriage. I was left to my thoughts again, day dreaming what may lye ahead of me, all the possibilities of what Asta, the 'psychic' could say. The train arrived at Northern-Star station and I walked the few blocks to Asta's house. She lived on Ocean Court, number 8. I always liked the number 8, it follows me —it's the infinity symbol and I lived at number 8 John Street.

I came to a little blue cottage with a nice garden surrounding it. There were strange ornaments scattered about the yard. I later discovered Asta believed they protected her and her house from unwanted spirits and guests (she scolded them later for letting me in). I pounded on the large white door loudly with the golden-octopus-door-knocker in the middle of her door. Instantly, the door opened and a short, pretty, tanned lady emerged from behind it. She had long sandy-blonde hair and kind lilac-blue eyes with flicks of yellow around her pupil and a tiny sparkle in her eye. She held a large piece of Selenite in her left hand. Asta kind of looked like a mermaid. She was smiling as though she already knew something —or, perhaps I was paranoid.

"Hello, Harlot!" she said happily before hugging me. "Come in, please, my reading room is right here"she said, gesturing to the small room next to the door with the Selenite.

I went in the 'reading' room and placed my belongings on a chair beside the door before sitting in a purple chair facing the window across from a blue chair. They were lovely chairs, comfortable and vintage; exactly what you would expect a fortune-teller to have. She had interesting, odd pieces of art and random tinctures everywhere. In the middle of the chairs stood a small table with a mint green sarong with little pictures of shells and fish draped over it. There were Tarot cards, tea-cups and a tea-pot already laid out on the table ready for the 'reading'. Asta sat in the chair opposite from me and began shuffling the deck before placing it back in the position it had been in before.

"Your hands please" she said, signalling me to put my hands into hers. "Ouch" she said, pulling her left hand away quickly and shaking it. She grabbed my hand again and turned it over, exposing my Peridot ring, "this ring is very old and there's a story behind it" she said, rubbing the small burn on her hand and leaning closer as she began talking to, and asking for guidance from, what she called, spirit. She was wrong, my Grandmother gave me this ring and she brought it brand new…I think… Actually I don't know..*I had just assumed.*

Asta took a deep breath in, and then started speaking at a rapid pace. "You feel lost, you're unsure of what is next and how in the world your life is ever going to get better" she looked up at me then continued talking before I could answer "I can sense you're feeling unfulfilled in all areas of your life, you don't just feel like something is missing, you feel like it's all missing, you feel like *you* are missing. It seems to me that you haven't really been who you truly are for your whole life, and you're fearful that if you were who you really are, you'd end up all alone —or in a mental institution" Asia stared at me, waiting for my response.

"Well" I slowly pondered the words to say, carefully, trying not to give her anything to manipulate or add on to, "I don't want my life to be the way it is, and who could blame me for that?" I said.

"You don't need to worry about that dear, I doubt you'll stay stuck much longer. Am I correct in saying you have been seeing your Grandmother lately?" Asta said.

"Nope, I haven't seen or heard from my Grandmother..Sometimes I think I can feel her but I know that's just nonsense and I'm letting grief get the better of me and give me false hope" I said.

"Oh dear. Denial speaking. Which is denial of who you really are Harlot, I know you've gone through some horrible experiences because of who you are but it is time now to allow yourself to be you, the world needs it, you need it and your gifts are beautiful. I promise, you are not an evil witch and these abilities are not from the devil.... I must let you know, if you don't accept yourself as you are and step into it, you'll be a very dark and angry person. I'm afraid that's the law of the universe, you signed a contract and took an oath before you entered this reality and it must be fulfilled…That's not to say that if you do chose your path you will have no darkness, there is a shadowy aspect, or a dark side of you. It is required to sustain equilibrium, it's because you can dive deep into the shadows, it gives you this spooky kind of feeling to others, much like that of a creature that dwells in the depths of the sea. Unheard of and unseen by the lands. *Undiscovered. Misunderstood. Different.* Intense? Yes —but certainly not evil… unless you want it to be. You can curse people at the drop of a hat, merely using your thoughts and the power of your words. You must understand, the power you yield is somewhat extreme, and I can tell you this, your ancestors do not like it when people fuck with or hurt you. Let them deal with it, and keep your pretty little hands clean. Oh dear child, you must know where you come from and who you are? You must know *something* mysterious happened to bring you here. Surely." Asta said.

"I guess maybe that could be true...not all of it, but maybe some.. maybe. I don't know. I do not know what to believe." I said

"There are a few others on the other side, some of whom have been around you since birth, others have come recently, the point is, they are patiently waiting, for you, to just be you.

Messages to loved ones are relying on you, sometimes there's a certain channel for those whom have passed on to come through. The beauty of identity crisis and of being unsure of yourself, not knowing who you are for so long, one becomes clear. A clear channel. See? It all has purpose. We have only wait for the time our misfortune shows the gift, when the time is right. It is a harsh way to learn, but how many great people have had it easy? Would *Marshall Mathers* have become *Slim Shady* without the shade?" She asked.

"Well, no.. but I don't think that makes it okay, why would I have chosen to live like this, I'm broke, I'm alone, I feel like shit and I've been diagnosed with a mental illness" I said, she ignored me and gave me a blank look.

For a moment there was silence, I sat there thinking: *'man this bitch really can talk some shit'*. She was waiting for me to speak. She shook her head.

"Oh. Pish. Tosh. You're not crazy. In the future it will be mainstream science, before long everyone will be into it to, then you'll be sorry you didn't take the initiative to go with what you knew to be true...Your Grandmother wants to tell you something. She tried to communicate with you when she was in her last days at the hospital, am I right??" She said.

"Ahh. No. What do you mean?"

"She opened her eyes *really* wide at you, remember? And you said to her, 'Nan, what are you doing', your mum said 'its Harlot' to which she said, 'I know that, I was just seeing who she really was'.. I know this freaked you out a little bit, but it shouldn't have. You need to see your spiritual talents as a gift, instead of a curse. Hmm, how can I put this?...we all have psychic abilities, just like we all have the ability to kick a football, but that doesn't mean we are all going to be professional football players." With that she stopped talking for a moment and left the silence to do its work... Honestly I thought she was even more nuts than me. Before too long, Asta started to speak again.

She seemed to love the sound of her own voice, I suppose I was paying her to speak.

"Oh, and theres a boy"

"there's no boy" I said ..

"yet" she said with a little smile on her face. I couldn't help but notice the little twinkle in her eye. I didn't like feeling like she knew more than I did. "He has some kind of symbol tattoo on wrist consisting of triangles and circles, he's very strong and hard working, he follows his heart, he's different too, and he is open to all this stuff so no need to worry there. It will feel very comfortable, like coming home, you'll be able to discuss things you have never said out loud before, things you won't even write down."

When she said this, the bracelet my Nan had left me came to mind. My Grandfather was a Taurus, and quite romantic, he had gifted my Grandmother a bracelet with a band of hearts and two larger size hearts that he'd engraved their initials in script (before they'd made it offical, mind you). What is odd is the initials in one heart looked like mine. Deep into old age my grandparents always held hands. The little things matter to me. Virgo, yeah?

"….Although Harlot, and I want to make this very clear, you do not, in any sense of the word, *need* him. I do not want you to waste your time looking for 'the one', or waiting for some boy to come along and complete you, or come and save you, he will come when you are ready, when you know who you are, when you are who you are meant to be, when you accept yourself and can stand on your own two feet alone. Get it?? "

"Yes, I understand" I said to Asta, though I knew I never wanted a relationship. I do not trust men.

"O.K. Good enough for me…It's a good thing, you know, to help others with their pain, but remember, you must deal with your own first" Asta said readying the tea-leaves and shuffling her Tarot deck. She placed both on the table, dividing the cards, then slowly running her left hand above the tea-cup and the cards, then back again.

Her movements were very strange, almost non-human, she moved like a fish swimming through water. Her eyes were closed and she was breathing slowly. She picked up her selenite wand and waved it over the cards, the teacup, herself and then got up to move it around me.

I sat, flabbergasted with everything that she'd said to me thus far, I was sure she was full of it. She needed therapy much more than me and that made me feel good and sane… I waited for Asta to return to reality.

"Tea leaves first!" she said, startling me as she broke the confusion I sat in.

The only noise had been the large Grandfather clock, tick-ticking proudly in the corner of the room next to the fire place. She had tea-pots and tea-cups everywhere, as if I'd been invited the *Mad Hatter's* tea-party. I had been so engulfed with her strong presence, I hadn't noticed all the little quirky details in her interesting, and weird house.

She walked over to the mantle of the fireplace and picked up a white tea-cup with gold polka dots "Ah, this one! Of course, this is the one" she said, so loud she was almost shouting. She tilted the teacup on its side, leaving a dead dragonfly sitting on the saucer. "Umm, may I ask what the dragonfly is for??" I asked, trying not to sound arrogant. Truthfully I was thinking 'what the fuck, this lady is strange, she's stranger than anyone I've ever met, stranger even than me.' I felt so normal around her. "It's lucky" she said with a matter-of-fact tone, "this is a very special tea-cup, I've been waiting a long time for the person I would get to use it with" Asta said, with a I-know-something-you-don't-kind-of-smile plastered on her face, a look I was becoming very familiar with — and it was irritating the hell out of me. She placed the teacup and saucer, with the 'lucky' dragonfly on it in front of me. Asta turned to grab something behind her and returned holding a floral tea-pot with with steam seeping out the spout, and a black and blue feather stuck in the little steam hole on its lid. It was now I realised how many feathers she had around in all different colours and sizes. "Where did you get the tea-pot from? And what on earth are all the feathers for?" I said. I'd spoken abruptly, without considering her feelings, my thoughts written across my face. "You do ask a lot of questions. A very curious child indeed" she said.

I found her calling me child creepy, as she looked to only be a few years older than me herself. Her self-confidence in what she believed in was inspiring.

The power of smoke and mirrors.

Asta put the tea leaves in my white and gold tea cup and poured hot water on top at a relaxed pace. I stared to and fro between her and the tea, trying to make sense of what was going on.

"Drink." Asta ordered.

It took some time for me to drink all the tea as it was too hot. Eventually I got it all down, leaving the tea-leaves at the bottom of the tea-cup. I placed the tea-cup back on the gold and white polka-dot saucer.

Asta seemed to be oozing with excitement as I finished the tea. She grinned widely from ear to ear, eerily like the *Cheshire Cat*. "Now what do you see, dear?" Asta said, gesturing towards the tea-cup. I leant forward to peer into the cup. I was right —just a bunch of damp tea leaves. Asta took the cup. She said she could see an array of images. First, a wolf, standing alone. She told me, this was a symbol of myself, a symbol of what I was destined to be, apart from the flock, creating my own path. A crow, a symbol of connection from other worlds to this one, submerging the veil from past, present and future. She said a cat jumped out at her, transforming into a jaguar, a creature of the night, a symbol of shamanism to the Mayan culture, which was apparently a big deal to her.

A man in a hat presented himself —she was unable to make out whether it was a top-hat or a cowboy hat but she felt I knew this man.. a long time ago.

A village appeared vividly, as if not only a picture in tealeaves, she leaned the cup forward to show me. It was no ordinary village. A mystical and unusual place, like nowhere I'd ever seen, not even on a movie, there were little people with wings darting around — much like the movements of a dragonfly."What do you see?" Asta questioned. "A…a fairy kingdom…I think…" Somehow, the image was moving, the winged people were going about their day unaware they were being watched —from another land..in tea cup. It couldn't be real. I looked up at Asta and she froze, as if she had just seen a ghost —although I assumed she would be used to that sort of thing. I felt someone tap my shoulder, trying to get my attention to look out the window. As I turned my head looking out the large double windows, a murder of crows surrounding a lady in a red dress with bright-blue eyes and blonde hair. A lady I had seen a few times befor, briefly —from the corner of my eye. She had a wolf sitting beside her, with the same bright-blue eyes. The wind powerfully blowing her hair away from her face.

13 crows, a wolf, and *her*, staring at me. Staring into my soul.

Why was she following me? Who was she?

My eyes locked with hers. The entire world disappeared.

There was something she needed to tell me.

I could sense it.

The intensity of her glance was too much.

I glanced at the Grandfather clock. It read 3 o'clock…

Still?…I looked out the window and the lady, the wolf and the crows had all vanished. Disappeared into thin air. Maybe, it didn't really happen…I hope. I'm having delusions again. Asta was still frozen. *Why wasn't she moving? Or talking, she loved to talk. A moment ago I couldn't get her to shut up.* The clock was no longer ticking. My body felt heavy and dense. It was hard to move. I had to check the time. *Where was my phone?* I pulled myself from the vintage blue chair while Asta sat perfectly still and frozen in time. I reached my bag at the entry of the 'reading' room that had been sitting on top of another chair, next to an old chest covered in pillows. I found my phone in the mess of useless crap covering the bottom of my handbag.

3 p.m. Strange.

Asta may have another clock inside her cottage. I tried to move as fast as I could but my body was stiff and rigid —like dead weight. Finally I reached her kitchen after what felt like hours down the short hallway. There was a large clock black and white, roman numeral clock hanging above her sink.

3 p.m. Can't be.

That isn't possible. All I wanted was my damn fortune read, maybe some answers. It's just cards and tea-leaves. This has to be some kind of joke she's playing on me because I think this stuff little silly…Well, okay, I think it's fucking ridiculous nonsense, but seriously..Come on. It is. She's messing with me. I know it. She has to be responsible for this.I bet she's moved by now. How long have I been standing here, staring at this clock, talking to myself? I felt fearful, which quickly turned to anger, rising up and coursing through my veins like fire. Shit.This crazy bitch is getting a piece of my mind. It's so hard to move. My feet feel as if they are covered in concrete, limbs as if I'd been lying on them for hours on end and they had gone to sleep. Numb. *How could she be doing this? A curse? Some kind of black magic..* must be —but magic isn't real. I swear I heard giggling coming from that end of the cottage. What an odd laugh. It was what you'd expect a mischievous little elf's chuckle to sound. *Why did I come here?* I should have known better than to get involved in things like this. This is not good for my mental health. What do dragonflies know anyway? What business do they have carrying a mentally-ill woman's business cards around. Things can be just coincidences. I thought this would just be a bit of fun, a good laugh, that for sure I'd be able to cross this stuff off and throw it in the looney bin — where it belongs. I was growing more and more annoyed as I crawled closer to the room I had left Asta in. Crawling seeming to be the fastest form of transportation at this point. I felt normal — closer to the ground, apart from the fact that I was crawling. When I arrived to the 'reading' room, Asta was still there, sitting completely still, with the same look on her face as when I had left the room. "Oi! ….Hey?!…Lady. That's enough now. You can stop. Joke's over!!It's not funny anymore" I yelled closely to her face. She didn't even budge, not in the slightest —no smirk, no movement, no reaction at all. She wasn't blinking or breathing… not at all. This has to be some kind of cruel trick. She's a trickster and this is trickery. That's what I had to tell myself at this point anyway..I was very confused what the right move was now. None of this made any sense. I tried to stay calm and sat back down, across from Asta, hoping that maybe, just maybe, she might come back. In the moment my backside hit the chair, she took a giant gasp of air and then began panting profusely and then skulled her glass of water.

"Ahh, Asta? What the hell just happened??" I said, my eyes set on her, demanding an explanation.

"I knew. I just knew. As soon as I laid eyes on you and looked into those damn supernaturally bright-baby-blues. You're not from here. I can't say too much more. I've already told you too much. They won't allow me to say anything more, hence the stopping the clock and freezing time.

You must figure out your course on your own, that's the way it *has* to be. I can remind you that you are guided and protected, and that you are never, nor will you ever be alone. Shit, theres an army of people behind you helping you. My advice to you would be to trust your gut, follow your heart, open your eyes, ears and to actually feel what is around you. Don't judge the messages you receive, but don't believe it all either, the trick is to decipher who is sending the messages to you. Let the animals point you in the right direction. You're so special. It's scary, you're something else, everyone can see it. Trust me, it is only you who doesn't see it. Now, you must leave." While speaking she had shuffled me out the front door. "Wait! Just tell me who 'they' are and what the hell I am? What do you mean?? Please?! I need answers, I have no clue what I'm meant to be doing" I said, my voice whiney —but I *was* desperate, so I didn't have a choice but to plea for help. "It's okay. You will figure it out eventually. Now go, please, this is too much! Everyone knows, you do not fuck with the fairies. Go! leave now!"

And she slammed the door in my face.

I spent the train ride home repeating and analysing everything that had happened, reviewing every last detail with a fine tooth comb as only a Virgo could, yet, no avail. What the fuck just happened? *Did she say fairies?*

***

I woke early the next morning and on my vintage blue-bicycle
with a basket in the front —much like the bike *Dorothy* rides in
the *Wizard of Oz* film, I headed to the Library. The basket was
great for carting books around. I regularly visit the Library, but
this day was as if I was being called there —similar to the walk I
felt I had to go on, the day the dragonflies swarmed me.
I am sure we only see what we want to see, hear what we want to
hear and feel what we want to feel, or at least we block certain
aspects of ourselves and the world around us until we are truly
ready.. until the time is right. I arrived at the Library and went to
the Philosophy section, next to the religion section. I had thumbed
through a couple of the books over the years —for a small town
they had a vast range of Philosophy books, I hadn't seen any of
the books I did that day —yet they felt familiar.
One book particularly stood out to me. *'The Red Door Prophecy'*
was written along the spine in gold lettering of an old, old, red-
leather book. I picked the book up and examined the cover.
I felt as if my hand and the book were magnets, pulling and
binding us together.
Suddenly, another book jumped out at me from the shelf and fell
onto the floor.
It too, was another book about *'The Red Door'*. I thought I would
maybe get some books on Psychics to help me figure out what
happened yesterday, but these books seemed to want to come with
me —like they kept information just for me. Obviously that's
crazy talk, but I just had a 'feeling'. More books jumped out at

me, then I had all I could carry. I borrowed the books and set off to read them.

27 was the number of books I took from the Library about *The Red Door society* that day. The limit of books one can borrow is usually 25, but the librarian let me take the extra because she knew I'd be back.

I put all the books in my basket, balancing them one on top of the last and carried the few that wouldn't fit. I set off to find a secluded spot down Scenic drive (where the dragonflies had swarmed me.) Unbeknownst to me at the time, I would uncover a deep and dark secret.

As far as I could grasp, with limited knowledge and tainted perspective, The Red Door is a secret society, hidden in plain sight, all around 'normal' society with a monumental amount of unpleasantry, illegal dealings and hidden authority in day to day life.

They disguise themselves as a bunch of drunken fools (which, mind you —many of them actually are) whilst preforming sacred, ancient rituals, sacrifices and performing unjust magic from the instructions passed down from the 'wizards' before them .. They call this their 'secret knowledge'.

The 'wizards' before them didn't invent the craft —but they sure as hell perfected black-magic and recorded it all in step by step format giving any Tom, Dick or Harry the power to replicate evil spells without half a brain or any understanding of what they were doing... Well, that is —as long as you sell your soul and pledge an undying alliance and loyalty to the 'brothers.' All the 'Dicks' had jumped on board, summoning demons and slaughtering animals or babies in hopes Satan would favour them. Blood rushed to my face in rage, my stomach riddled with anxiety, heart growing heavy realising who the people I'd grown up around really were. The problem is, once you know, you cant un-know. That is why sometimes it is better to not know; we don't know, what we don't know and ignorance is bliss.

I'm not one to stay blind, or to condone ignorance, but the pain of knowing the hard truths gives an understanding to why people choose to stay in denial for their lives and why we only see what we *choose* to see..

I had heard most, if not all, of this utter nonsense throughout my childhood, without ever fully comprehending what I was being told and defining it as 'normal'. Thats the thing about 'normal', it is whatever you are used to, and for me that was dark magic, negative thinking, and defiance of God's existence but sureness of the Devil's.

Apprently, the women were the masterminds behind it all. A select few chosen for 'who they are' —their genetic code and the blood they carry. A birth-right to the Red Door society.

The High Priestesses. The embodiment of Satan herself.

A specific bloodline filled with mystical gifts, passed down generation to generation. Encoded within the DNA holding the ability perform the hideous acts.

As I read and the information flooded my thoughts. Intricate and intertwining conclusions rushed by my minds eye. I experienced the sensation of 'de-ja-vu', like when B1 and B2 know what each other are thinking and the world starts shaking.

It was as if an instant download had inserted itself into my brains hard-drive. I remember telling myself, 'no, this cant be' aloud. I wanted to wipe it all away and sweep it all under the rug, to pretend I was paranoid and go back in time and un-know the things I now knew.

It would have been so easy, the ideas rolling about me were too extreme to hold any truth and sounded more like insanity.

I had seen all of the symbols in the books around town and inside my family home.

I'd witnessed the secret handshakes and seen 'hidden hand' gestures replicated in photographs. I tried to come up with any other reason for it all. Any possible reason why I had heard all of this doctrine all my life. It was impossible to logically lie to myself anymore.

There was no talking myself out of what was there, clear as day, right in front of my eyes. My family are the leaders of a cult. They'd kept me in the dark about their 'Red Door' secret my whole life…

Well.. *kind of.*

They'd manipulated me. Red Doors are renown for playing games with the truth —it's a learned skill. It seems they had been using the oldest trick the book, The Red Door book that is. Mind-manipulation, the sleight of hand or 'the hidden hand'.

The magicians favourite trick. To own a mind is to control reality. Who was to say what was real and what was fake at this point.

It was all a bit too much..My life is one big fat lie. They probably made my Psychologist diagnose me with schizophrenia so no-one would ever believe a word I said because whose gonna believe a crazy woman? An orchestrated hypocrisy of counterfeit bullshit.

As I learned more and more of the stories of the Red Door regime, my world collapsed around me.

The walls of what used to be fell in, and crumbled to dust.
Life-long blind spots emerged from the shadows to plague me and
metamorphosed the person I used to be —who I thought I was
and who I thought they were.
It was as if my brain was a machine exploding, an engine
overheating, a technologic malfunction.
The deep-sea of denial and dark areas in my subconscious brain
came rising up deteriorating old neural-pathways, forming new
connections at an unnatural iconic speed..
What is one to do upon finding out their world is a web of lies?
When all the people around you are in on it?
When the story that I've told and re-told myself each day are all
lies and scams?
What is one to do when the who I am, and what I am capable of,
changes in an instant?
Who the fuck am I... really?
I didn't have the slightest clue.
Do I want to know?
Past feelings of loneliness, guilt, shame, isolation and mistrust all
crept up to the surface slowly suffocating me.
Deep down I had always known I was different.
I have always been the black sheep.
The odd duck.
The scape-goat of my family and friends.
An outcast....but this was something else. I didn't think *this*.
The ability to lie to ones self can be a super power —and it makes
sense.
Failure to possess the viable components for basic human
connection and the brain will create a ball of twine full of coping

mechanisms to keep safe, or *Stockholm Syndrome*. Defined as: feelings of trust or affection felt in many cases of kidnapping or hostage taking by a victim towards a captor.

It's twisted and complex, but has a certainly has a haunting beauty to it.

Technically I hadn't been kidnapped but what happens when you are born into a family of sociopaths?

My hungry mind craved more knowledge and the truth.

The truth, the whole truth and nothing but the truth.

The power.

I looked through my library treasures and again. The book I'd seen first at the Library stood out to me again, as if it were screaming to be opened.

The book with the title *'The Red Door Prophecy.'* Underneath the title it read: A continuance of noble creed derived of the greatest legacy: The Moon Child.

The butterflies in my belly had grown so large I thought I'd throw up.

The need to know overtook my thought processing.

I'd already tried to deny it.

I thought: fuck it, and opened the book.

My heart was pounding loudly in my chest.

There was a mixture of stress and anxiousness —which honestly, beat the endlessness boredom I was used to experiencing.

Beneath the covers of the book I recited tales of rambles my drug-effected Father had repeated. I already knew it all.

It was simply a matter of remembering.

'The best way to hide something is to keep it in plain sight' speaks volume in Red Door culture.

Their mantra and safe guard, what would be their slogan.

I came to a part in the book titled: *'The High Priestess'*.

I skimmed pages that included descriptions of traits and attributes required and a detailed recollection of experiences, which, according to the book 'create a High Priestess'. The Red Door Society must perfect a ritual — a ritual performed while the mother is still with child. The ritual takes place in the moon-light during a rare planetary occurrence and then, there's a sacrifice, blood and chanting —while the 'Grand Master' reads an incantation to posses the unborn foetus. They call this baby 'the Moon-child', and it is the first initiation of the process to coming the High Priestess to run the wicked organisation.

It stated that prospective Priestesses must be unaware of what is going on —or, it will taint her innate power and gifts. She must find the answers for herself with no help from anyone else. She must suffer to conquer and overcome hardships to become a true master; after all it is an 'honour' that only happened once every couple of hundred years.

A test of her courage —meaning to possess a strong heart and strength of will. Mixed with the right blood (arranged marriages are common in The Red Door Society) and timing of the Moon cycle.

I wasn't sure whether to be mad or glad —finally I had a reason for my bleak and miserable upbringing.

Having purpose is great, but... *what if I don't want to be the high priestess?*

What if I don't want all that responsibly?

What if I don't want to be apart of the Red Door Society?

Apparently a choice I didn't have the right to make. I'd read earlier that once a family member 'sells their soul' to the Red Doors, the cult owned the bloodline forever.

The selling of the soul is an old and weird ritual carried out when someone wants to be an initiated 'first degree'.

A noose is placed around the initiates neck, he is then slashed at with a blunt knife and falls back into a group of Red Doors, whom catch him and lift him back up. To signify their re-birth and symbolise giving of the soul to the Red Door craft. In the Red Door —there's always symbolic meaning. Then, rites are read, usually in latin.

Well fuck that. No one was going to tell me what my life meant, who I had to be and what I had to be apart of. I was used to being a loner and I would continue with that.

A witch without a coven.

I would play their game and beat them at it.

I would play their game, *to be free.*

From here, the overwhelming state of emotions took charge and I went back to what I had always known, to the way I had always reacted. I do not like to be lied to, no-one does but it drives me literally to the brink of insanity. A lunatic comes out from the depths of the darkest parts of me. I let the anger consume me. In the moment of my rage, I could hear a voice, a man's voice, coming from inside my head, it said:

"Harlot, this is your Grandfather, all is not as it seems. I'm so sorry for what we did. I promise it will all work out. I will help you. I will tell you what to do."

And just like that, it was gone. The anger left my body and I was left with more questions and some answers. I knew I must play it cool or they'd harm, or try to kill me.. *again.*

New pathways connected like wildfire in my mind creating a new cognitive map for me to explore —a new path for me to travel. I suddenly knew things, things not written in the Red Door books. Secrets never to be written down and risking the chance of blabber mouths.

After that day, I obsessively tried to warn others of the Red Door society and their agenda, showing propaganda and book after book of evidence. Despite telling myself I'd play it cool and play the game —I couldn't.

Luckily, no-one listened and no-one gave a shit. Alas, I was labelled 'that crazy girl with the queer stories'. Three times different men offered me to be initiated into the Red Door society, "..but I'm a female? Red Door is an all male establishment" I said. "Exceptions can be made" they'd reply.

I was so clueless at this time, thinking I knew everything, and I was playing with fire.

Naturally I began to piss them off and the niceties were no longer. Seven times Red Door members threatened to kill me.

Which considering how valuable the 'Moon-child' is to the Red Door society shows how much I was threatening them. They knew they had to try to get of rid me, besides, in their mind they owned me anyway. I had no choice who I wanted to be. They'd completed the ritual and now I was ruining it for them. What if people began believing what I was telling them? Making me look crazy could only last so long. The truth always comes out in the end.

To be honest, it wasn't so much a 'look' anymore, I had gone mad. I wasn't actually mad, I was just behaving in a mad way due to the stress of finding out my family were servants of Satan and they'd sold my soul to the devil before I was born —PTSD. I was hearing voices —and not at all nice voices, the ones that tell you that you're worthless. The voices told me to kill myself, that I was all alone in a world I wasn't meant to be in the first place. I'd see shadow people, as clear as day, standing in front of me —a shadow man, wearing a top-hat would follow me. A few times he had a little boy with him and he would be holding his hand. He would stand still and watch me. The 'Night-Hag' would visit me in my sleep, paralysing my body, sitting on my chest and choking me so hard I couldn't scream, glued to the bed, feeding on my fear. Grey aliens with long bodies and big heads would appear out of no where and stand at the end of my bed in a pack of three and observe me.

If I had of read the entirety of the 'Moon-child' chapter I could have saved myself from what was next —but I didn't. If all of the future circumstances of your life and proof you're not normal — and never will be, were all written in a book. Would you read it? That book still sends shivers down my spine. Only God knows — or should I say, *Satan* knows where it came from.

All I know for sure is, I burnt it and threw it in the river the day I found it. It felt so evil. Interestingly, I have never received a notice, a late fee or heard anything about that book ever again — not from the library, and on my online searches nothing comes up — like it never existed.

I fell into a deep depression. I believed everyone around me when they told me I was crazy, that I didn't belong, that I shouldn't be here. Insecurities and lack of self-worth clouded my judgements, with moments of paranoia and odd behaviour ruining my already tainted reputation.

I responded to my painful emotions by doing what I had seen everyone around me doing. I turned to alcohol and then, to drugs. If you hadn't put two and two together yet, allowing yourself to be in altered states of consciousness isn't a very good idea when you're irritating a very powerful group of devil worshipping, demon summoners and vengeful warlocks and witches.

It's a whole step-up if you're the 'Moon-child' and your purpose (according to the Red Door society) —is to bridge the gap between this world and the underworld.

Curiosity killed cat, naivety was the sentence.

At this point I'm self-consumed in misery, not playing it safe, basically asking for trouble. I just didn't care anymore. A part of me wanted it. I was thirsty to know what I really am and what I could handle. You couldn't ask for help where I'm from.. maybe that's just the way it is, and always has been.

Look picture perfect and pretend to be happy, no one really cares how you feel or what you have to say.. You're depressed? Get over it, go to work and solider on.

I came home one night after heavily drinking —in hysterics. It was Tuesday so all my family had gone out. They say like attracts like, so in my low state, I was vulnerable to psychic attack and possession by ill willed entities. When you're depressed, you are an easy target to anyone with sick intentions and malicious fantasies. I might as well of got red paint and drawn a target on myself. I was highly intoxicated and full of negative emotions, incredibly susceptible to the energies floating around me. Add too much of a depressant to mix, and you could be victim to mind control.A demon created by the people I had enraged took control of the drivers' seat, my will to live disappeared and I wanted out. I sat on the edge of my bed, crying. My heart weighing a tonne. A stabbing sensation piercing my throat, the grief pouring into my lungs making it difficult to breath.

I fell to the floor, unable to get up, pierced to the ground from the gravity of self-loathing. I could sense dark, evil energy around me. I could hear the people in my life saying, *she's faking it, just asking for attention.* The pain of my life experiences thus far, and the uncertainty of my life too much to chew. I had lived a life of constant insults, belittlement and abuse. Beaten down and beaten up. A slur of insults living in my memory rushed from my hippocampus to be played on repeat in my mind, like a swell of slimy quick sand, pulling me deeper into my pit of misery.

Fat, ugly, brail face,
evil witch,
crazy, weirdo,
fucking stupid cunt,
little bitch (my nick-name growing up),
dirty slut,
whore,
I don't know why I even had you,
fucking liar, rat,
you make shit up and no-one will believe a word you say, you're always starting shit, causing fights, you have no friends and there's literally not one person on the earth that wants you around. You're not good enough and you'll never amount to anything, no-one gives a fuck if you're alive or dead...

I began to see visions of myself, sitting alone in my room, reading books to escape and leave my reality behind —to try to feel like I was someone else, lying to people about what I did during the holidays and on weekends so they didn't know what was going on inside my home. I saw myself hating my body and everything about my personality, changing my hair colour every week trying to find —or to change who I was. I saw my eating disorder and other kids teasing me for being weird and having a face that is too round, eyebrows to thick and dark, for being poor and having holes in my school shoes and clothes (my family had money, but not for me)All my social awkwardness and failures.

I saw past relationships of dirtbag after dirtbag, cheating and lying.

I re-lived the moment of my Father beating me in a drug-fuelled rage, chasing 14 year old me around the dining table, grabbing the back of the head and dragging me by my hair to the cellar, smashing my head into the floor and pressing his knee into my head, squeezing it into the ground, screaming at me that I'm piece of shit, his face fire-engine red with blue veins popping out of his bald head. He kept me locked down there for a week, with no sunlight and just enough food and water to survive. The side of my head was bruised and my ear bled for a few days. This wasn't the most violent of his explosions, but this one sticks out in my mind because it happened on Christmas Eve. (If I ever confronted him, he'd say: "but did I molest you? You should be grateful to have a father like me." —No, you didn't molest me. Good on you for not fucking your children. Father of the year award goes to you.)

I felt the pain of the world, of past hurts and betrayals from best friends turned enemies and family to foe. All this came to me in the blink of an eye and the emotion overwhelmed me like a tsunami.I began chanting "kill me, kill me now" over and over again. I'd had enough, this world has too much pain and my life is too tragic.

In my minds eye as clear as day, as if I was watching a movie of the future; I saw myself going out into the kitchen, grabbing the big butchers knife, and slashing my both wrists vertically.

No note.

Bleeding out in the kitchen to be found in the morning.

I said out loud: "Fuck it. I'm doing it." I got up off the edge of the bed and charged ahead to go out of my room into the kitchen — but I couldn't get through the door way…What I can only describe as a force field, or a barrier of energy, stopped me from getting out of my room and going to the kitchen to slit my wrists that night. Instantly I turned around, got onto the bed and went to sleep. Out like a light in a split second.

I owe my life to a dog. My girl Daisy, didn't leave my side throughout the entire ordeal. My dog —and some weird force-field.

The next day I packed some of my personal belongings, (whatever would fit into my car)and with Daisy, drove 30 hours across the country in hopes of starting fresh and leaving who I was behind. I had been saving money to get out for a while but it didn't last long. I had no choice, so I went back..My whole life thus far, had been shit and I didn't want to add homeless and starving to the list. I was only gone for two weeks.

Slowly drowning, sinking lower and lower into the brink of insanity, trying my best not to drown as they watched, pushing my head further under water for their own sick amusement and pleasure. As they say, misery loves company.

I hadn't escaped yet, and I realised you cannot run from your problems, I would face the music. I would no longer fear them and I would not run away ever again.

I told myself I was not stuck with them; they were stuck with me. Through all this, my sprit refused to fully give up, and I began to find ways to get on my feet. My depression exhausted me, depleting my energy but I forced myself to get out of bed each morning. I started getting my health in order, I gave up the drink and started eating well, exercising, stretching and resting. I began researching and finding ways to emotionally heal.

It did not fix everything, but it helped me to gain some hope, and sometimes that is all you need to survive.

I decided getting creative might help me get it out — in a healthier way. I used to love to draw and paint when I was a kid, it helped me to forget all the shit and *be*.

The world would quiet and become only me, a piece of paper and pencil. Coincidently, on one of my trips to the Library I stumbled across a flyer for an art class that they held weekly. I cannot recall the name of the art teacher now, although I do vividly remember his dark-blue eyes, and the silver-star ring he wore. He was a cliché art teacher, unusual with a different way of thinking to most. His philosophy: everyone is an artist, all that was needed was to step out of the logical to the creative side of the brain and it would come all flowing out. He'd say a little imagination can go a long way, then he'd quote *Albert Einstein: 'Imagination is more important than knowledge'*.

He was constantly coming up with tips and tricks to get through to the 'inner child' and fire up the kid within. As with every class, we were given homework.

His assignment was to find the beauty in all things throughout our daily lives. Beauty is in the eye of the beholder and such.

Burdened by the silly assignment I took a stroll down Scenic Drive and sat against a large gum tree. I stared at another smaller tree that could barely be called a tree. It was more like a stick growing out of the ground with a couple of tiny branches and a few average looking leaves desperately holding onto the ends of them. I sat leaning against the neighbouring tree trunk and tried to look 'beyond' the appearance of the little tree and find the beauty within. My art teacher had told me it was inherit in all things, great and small.

While I studied every nook and cranny of this less than appealing couple of sticks stapled together posing as a tree I started feeling irritated again, letting off a chain reaction and I could feel the anger of yesteryear; except this time I didn't react, I stayed still, staring at the tree, leading me to think, 'what if that was the beauty I was supposed to see?' then I realised I was just thinking out my ass. He had said: stare at anything long enough and either, it will transform or it will transform you. Either way, the underlying beauty will inevitably reveal itself in every being, living or dead.

I couldn't help but feel jibbed.

What a load of shit.

I decided I'd stay a little longer and at least enjoy the fresh air and the sounds of nature for a while. Something about this place helped me to feel at peace, the serenity calmed me. That in itself could be seen as a blessing, so at least the trip wasn't a complete waste.

That moment, the exact second I gave up on seeing anything spectacular it occurred, I *saw it*. The once less than average looking leaves were all lit up and little illuminated flowers blossomed and covered the skinny branches then running up and down to the base of the trees trunk —but as fast as it had appeared, it stopped.

I quickly forgot about the light covered tree noticing a door on the ground, behind the tree. I was sure it would have caught my eye earlier as it was bright red.

True to nature, curiosity got the best of me.

I moved so quickly I basically levitated to the door —forgetting that there may be serpents sunbathing in the long green grass.

As I neared the bright red door I noticed it was surrounded by a circle of little mushrooms. The door had a pretty gold door handle, iridescent windows with images of dragonflies in them.

The windows were too thick to see through and the reflected the light in special way —much like a rainbow mirror, on steroids.

Under the handle was a little square key hole.

It was such a magnificent door to be plonked, smack-bang in the middle of the bush.

I wondered what it was doing here.

It was a door fit for the entrance of a multi-million-dollar mansion.

I reached down and tried to lift the door up off the ground, unable to get firm grasp.

It was as if the door was plastered into the floor of the woods.

Next, I'd tried to open the handle.

Locked.

I tried to look through the windows. No prevail. It was useless.

Something told me to try my peridot ring in the keyhole of the door… for a laugh I complied.

I almost fainted when it was a perfect fit and unlocked the door, making the handle moveable.

Somehow during my fiddling and thumping around the door had changed positions.

The door was now standing up-right…

It's funny looking back. How one second can define your life, and quite comical that we don't see these choices coming or realise how defining and detrimental they are until much later down the track. The second passed, and in the midst of my pondering and questioning I had already moved through the doorway.

I had no idea where I was. My phone wasn't working, so there was no chance of Google Maps helping me verge my way through the unknown territory.

To the eye, it looked exactly the same as where I had been standing before —but it *felt* different.

I felt lighter and free, without a care in the world.

The colours looked brighter, everything had a little sparkle, a captivating twinkle, shimmering as if glitter had been thrown all through the air. I turned to reinspect the door, maybe find a few answers or…something. I could see through the windows on this side of the door, I could see where I was just standing, except now I was looking from above. This didn't make sense, I was right way up but the door appeared to be lying on the ground again while I gazed through the windows. A dragonfly zoomed past my peripheral vision, I turned my head to follow it. Crickets sung loudly. I could sense magic in the air.

I turned my head towards back towards the door. It had vanished, without a trace and I was left in an unfamiliar place, puzzled.

Where had the door gone? And where was I?

Little did I know, I was leaving the real world far behind.

The desire to explore overrode the anxiety and worry I should have been feeling, given the circumstances. I had no idea how I would get home, yet for some reason —I felt completely safe with a distant feeling of familiarity. I had been here before.

I knew this place…

The colours of the flowers, trees and butterflies were the most vivid beautiful hues I'd ever seen.

Colours not even on the spectrum. I don't think the English language has the names to describe the brilliance of the unusual hues and tones.

I chased a pair of dragonfly to a dazzling water-stream a few hundred metres north from where my journey had began. I think it was north anyway.

The water was gorgeous and enticingly inviting.

Before I knew it, I'd removed my clothing and dove into the clear pool of water.

The water was refreshing. It felt like it was rejuvenating and rewinding every single cell of my body, removing all the damage and negativity from my energy field.

I don't know how long I'd been swimming and enjoying the entrancing water before I heard menacing giggling from the bank —the same laughter I had heard at Asta's (the psychic lady's house) when time had stopped. I tried to swim as fast as I could manage to get out of the water and re-dress myself.

Something tugged on my hair. I spun around to see what had pulled my hair.

Nothing there.

I started swimming towards the bank again. Another tug of my hair. I stopped, turned and water sprayed in my face —a stream water being spat at me. I rubbed my eyes clear. A woman with half her face was immersed below the water, her turquoise eyes shining like magnificent gems. Her eyes had tiny golden flicks near the pupil of her eye. They reflected so clearly onto the water I was seeing four of her lovely ocean green-blue eyes. Her red hair floating around her like silk, as if she was shooting a shampoo commercial. She wasn't wearing any clothing.

"Ahh, um, who are you?" I nervously splattered words together.

With a mischievous and cheeky laugh, she lifted her mouth from out of the water and shot a stream of water into my face again. I wiped my eyes, *again.* She was smirking and looked pleased with herself.

"Who are you??" I demanded. She giggled and said "my name is Aphrodite. Fairy of the water. Nymph of the wetlands. A mermaid. A siren. Whatever you want to call it, that's what I am.."

"A mermaid!?" I repeated, in disbelief.

Aphrodite lifted her tail-fin out of the water and gave me a wave with it. This made me lightheaded, and very overwhelmed.

I laughed uncontrollably at the improbability of what I was seeing, while sinking to the bottom of the glorious water.

I vaguely remember Aphrodite taking me out of the water but the sight of her fish tail pulled me into unconsciousness again and I fainted for a second time.

Sometime later, I woke. In shock and unsure of what I'd seen, and questioning if it had happened at all.

Once I had fully opened my eyes fully, I knew it had really happen.

There were three very beautiful human-like creatures standing over me, human but with wings…humans don't have wings. Their beauty was mesmerising, like nothing I had ever seen. Their faces had a few imperfections, one of the girls teeth were yellowish, the boy had lots of freckles and the other girl was really pale —but added to their charm. They seemed so confident and at peace with themselves exactly as they were.

I stood staring at these amazingly gorgeous people, pondering what they were. Then I remembered I had been naked. I looked down at my body. Luckily, I was wearing clothing. I wasn't sure who'd dressed me, or if the three beautiful winged people had seen my naked body but the clothes I was wearing weren't mine, so I guess they must have. I was wearing a pretty green dress, much like a dress you'd imagine Tinker-bell from Peter Pan to be wearing. A 'pixie' dress.

"Oh, good! You're finally awake" the male of the group said.

"Um, yeah..but why do I feel so…*different*?" I said.

"Ah, yes" the boy said "well, that could have something to do with hours you spent in the Lake of youth and wisdom, or, perhaps that hickey on the side of your neck may offer some explanation.." He said. "Hickey?! What? How could I have a hickey??" I asked

The dark-haired female of the group chimed in before the others could speak

"Aphrodite. The siren. Fairy of the water. She's a nymph and that's just what they do. Sirens are very..let's say, playful. If you weren't of Fairy blood, you'd be much worse off then you are now…though, you wouldn't even be in our world if you weren't.. That water would dissolve every last fibre of a human…Anyway.. Don't worry about it, your cells are just catching up to the rewinding process, much like an old tape being rolled back with a pencil and the sexual encounter will bring a lot of insight —soon it will all have been a gift" she said quickly.

"A gift?? How on earth do you propose being taken advantage of a gift?..And, of fairy blood? What does that mean?? What's fairy blood" I said. I couldn't get my questions out quick enough. I wanted answers.

"Well, I mean, you were basically parading yourself around her naked, what do you expect?" The boy said with a sarcastic tone.

I dismissed his comment, preoccupied by the things that the dark-haired girl had mentioned. "Fairy blood?" I questioned, again.

The sandy-blonde girl spoke. "We don't have time to discuss such a matter here. God only knows who may be watching… and listening. We ought to get a move on, we're late, someone very important would like to see you. It's about time you showed up." Her voice was gentle but direct.

"Who would like to see me? How do they know I'm here?" I said.

"Come now, follow me please, I'll lead the way —we're heading west" she said, with a smile and kind eyes, before turning to walk down a path I'm not sure was there before.

Something about these strangers made me want to follow whatever command they gave me.

Their eyes spoke so loudly, it was irresistible. I felt like they were communicating with my soul. I stood staring at the three beautiful people wondering to myself what they were. Obviously what they've said *can't* be true. It's impossible. Humans do not have wings nor do they have fish tails, and water doesn't rewind cells —and yet, here we are.

We walked for some time through the lovely bush-land, until eventually we arrived at a little town…

Everyone in the town had their own set of wings, every colour and different shapes, each set unique from the previous. They were all so stunning. Their wings were lovely but their brightly coloured eyes were the real stand out —like a gem had been captured inside their iris, so bright and sparkling, filled with light. Their skin was flawless and effortlessly beautiful. Each had their own imperfection and this added to their deep beauty and grace, they came across humble and confident, breathtaking but down to earth. Their eyes and wings always matched colours.

I was in a place of true beauty and glamour, without a trace of fakery or debauchery. A home-coming and feeling of relief rushed my senses. I continued looking around like an excited child. Throughout the town, animals roamed free, there was as many animals as there were fairies walking about the valley. "Is that…Is that a unicorn??" I asked. The boy turned to face me before stating, "Of course! What? You don't have them where you come from?" He slightly lifted the corner of his mouth to a sneer before looking ahead, leaving me to admire the mystical creature. "Hello friend!"

I reached my arm out to grasp the boys shoulder, "Who said that Did you say that?" I asked.

"What? Me? No. That was Alfred, your new unicorn friend" the boy was grinning ear to ear like the Cheshire cat as he spoke.

"Animals can't talk and unicorns are not real."

"What an odd thing to say. Of course animals can talk. My! What arrogance. You must apologise at once!" Alfred said.

"Umm, sorry Mr. Unicorn…Alfred..I'm..err…not from here and I've never met a unicorn before, especially not one as fabulous as yourself" The unicorn tilted his head before throwing it back in a great bout of laughter. His long luscious colourful mane flowing in the breeze. "You'll remember soon enough" Alfred said, before happily galloping away.

The houses were made of glass and I could see into their homes. All the little roads were formed from magnificently tumbled gems and stones. A crystal walkway that felt like fluffy cotton candy under my heels. The energy from the rocks coursed up and down my body. I felt that I'd become a whole different person energetically by being here. They told me that in the valley anything and everything one desired or conjured up in could manifest. 'Be careful what you wish for' they warned.

Zing!

In the blink of an eye I was holding an ice cream cone. A chocolate wafer cone with old-english-toffee scoops of ice-cream beaming from the sides of the cone. I find it funny now that the first thing that came to mind after being told I could have anything in the whole universe, all I had to do was conceive the idea —a simple ice cream cone was number one. Next I decided I needed an outfit. In an instant I was surrounded by rows of shoes and expensive garments made of the best materials. It was the closet of my dreams. I picked out a pair of beautiful black high-heeled boots, black skinny jeans, a black silk t-shirt and a black leather jacket. I completed the look with black sunglasses, bright red lipstick and nail polish to match.

It was my *Sandy* moment and I felt like a badass.

Now, I wanted to have fun and do something cool.

Suddenly I was swirling in a sea of colour, spinning around a drain of rainbow. Round and round until I landed in a place of madness, much like *Dorothy* landing in *Munchkin-Land*. If a circus and *Disneyland* had a baby —it would be this place. Horns sounded and glitter shot from thin air. There were bunnies and pictures of clowns hanging on the trees. This place made no sense at all and I wondered who could possibly imagine up all of this. It was all much, *too much.*

"FUN! - WE MUST HAVE FUN!!' Someone yelled from the distance. A woman dressed in a colourful suit (like something *Willy Wonker* or the *Mad-Hatter* would wear — with more colour.) She had rainbow glitter eye shadow and bright pink lipstick, with glitter through her white-blonde hair, topped with a purple top-hat and a baby-blue feather. She was enticing and interesting to look at —there was different elements to her style that jumped out at you the longer you looked. "Hello! How do you do?" She said with a big bright smile. "I would have prepared a fun activity if I knew you were coming, nobody ever tells me anything around here..never mind, I suppose I can conjure something fun for us to do..hmmm…" she said, trailing off, looking into the sky. In an instant a carousel sprang into existence. It was sparkly and had dancing rainbow unicorns prancing around the circle.

"What are you waiting for? Hop on, we're going on an adventure" she said. Mesmerised by the sight of the carousel I did as she said —without realising I had no information about this woman and essentially I was 'going on an adventure' with a strange woman I knew nothing about.

"Where are we going" I asked. "Where ever we want to!!" She said, clapping her hands in an odd rhythm. With the sound of her clapping the carousel began spinning faster and faster until I could no longer see what was around me, it all become a cloud of colourful glitter.

A whirlwind of fantasy spewed into the wind. We landed in an aircraft high above the clouds. "You always wanted to fly? Yes?….Not like this? Okay" and in an instant the aircraft disappeared and we each sprouted wings. Really big angel wings. Blue and purple filled the sky. We went higher and higher, gliding above the clouds. It was easy to steer and the wings flew along without much effort.

"Okay, what's the next 'wildest dream' you've ever had" she said condescendingly "to travel at the speed of light?" Wild dream after wild dream, from invisibility, eating endless amounts of burgers and cotton candy, dancing on the moon and playing all kinds of instruments without any practice or know-how, we carried out all of my fantasies. Every crazy thought I'd ever dreamt since I was a kid, and while they were fun in the moment; at the end of it all, I didn't feel how I thought I would feel if I'd possessed these abilities, or did these things when I dreamt of them. The woman became kind of intense, which was strange because I didn't even know her first name, or anything else about her… only that she liked to have fun, all the time, non-stop. It was exhausting. Sitting in the midst of this wild wonderland, on a bench made of candy-canes and glitter, we finally had time to rest. "May I ask what is your name?" I said. She didn't respond. She was looking down, zoned out in her own little world. I wondered what thoughts she might have, what did she do when she was here all alone? Was it still fun? "I don't know anything about you, would you like to tell me something about yourself? Hopefully we can get to know each other a little better" I said.

Again, she ignored me. It occurred to me that she may not have a real personality, or even be able to hold a simple conversation after all the fun…like a come-down, there was nothing left inside her. She'd tapped out her serotonin and sat still —like a robot out of battery. An empty party girl. I couldn't help myself, I had to try again " has anyone ever tried to get to know you..the _real_ you?"

"No." she said. I was happy to get a reply. "Will you tell me your name?" I asked.

"I don't know my name, no-one ever gave me one, and no-ones ever asked, so I didn't bother making one up.." She said.

"No name?" I asked. _The nameless fun one…_ there was a silent sadness behind her eyes, the kind of sadness felt by those that don't know themselves. Those that feel unknown by the whole world, including themselves. What kind of loneliness must one feel, if they're stranded on an island alone without even the company of their inner self… or at a party, surrounded by people that cannot see them. They say the eyes are the looking glass to the soul, but what happens when people look in your eyes and see nothing, they see right through you, because you don't know who you are.

"It's fine, I'm fine. What else can we do that's FUN? We must have fun" she said, standing up "I must go, there are things to do, I do not like to talk about such things, I must keep moving, I must have fun" and she ran off disappearing into the skyline, without turning to wave goodbye or look back at me. I never did learn her name, or get to know a thing about her, we had a fun and a slightly exhausting experience, and then as quickly as she had come, she'd gone…

"Careful" the winged boy said as I snapped back to their reality, "if you don't know where you're going, or what you want, you'll end up places you'd rather not be; trust me."

I decided the little things; soothing the soul by means of the senses could be more fulfilling than grand gestures of fun and that sometimes the fun one, is sad, trying to keep busy enough to forget, busy enough to not be known, and not have anyone see their true sadness.

"The king!!The king is coming!" all the winged people called filling the air with a buzz of electricity in the air from their excitement, while they darted around erratically, the way dragonfly do, their wings glimmering in the light of the Moonshine. They told great stories of their king, the ruler of this strange and peculiar place.

The king arrived wearing no shoes. A barefoot king..

Immaculately and impeccably dressed —minus the shoes to complete his attire. His feet were the cleanest, and most manicured feet I'd ever seen. I am still unsure why this stuck out in my mind, I just felt there was some importance to it. How often does one encounter a barefoot king?

Why was he wearing no shoes?

The words blurted out of my diaphragm. No greeting or anything, I said straight out "why are you wearing no shoes?….uhh, your majesty…Sir."

The barefoot king grinned at me, with his friendly sparkling eyes. He had yellow flicks through his green iris, bordering his pupil.

Instant relief breezed through my body and the tension fell away the moment we made eye contact.

"Follow me please, dear child, I would like to give you something; we can chat along the way" the Barefoot King said. I felt a sort of familiar comfortability emanating from him. I knew this man, I didn't know how, but I knew, I know him.

He was a warm and fuzzy fellow —how you'd imagined Santa Claus to be, but his physical appearance was more like a surfer or hippie. He had honey-blonde hair down to his broad shoulders and an infectious smile. In a way, being around him, made Santa feel real again. "Can I tell you a tale of tautology while we stroll? He asked. "I want to paint a picture in your mind —using words, to take you on an adventure of the mercurial persuasion, riding the unpredictable yet whimsical waves of past history, future prospects, the general consensus, an essential prerequisite, unusual and usual habits, new innovations, the pattern of opinion, free gifts and the almighty revolutionary soul evolving wisdom born from simplicity" he paused for a moment. "Are you ready for Mercury, our planet of communication to change your life?... To learn the significance of communication and nobility of a simple conversation?" He said.

"Er, yeah, I think so" I said, still pondering his speech. I had never met anyone who spoke in the manner he did. Honestly, I thought it was quite odd and hard to comprehend.

"Firstly, did your grandma ever tell you about the Mail-man?" He asked.

"As a matter of fact, she did, a little. It was a curious story —although I've never really thought too much of it, apart from the obvious questions, how did he find them and where did the people sending the letters address them?" I said. "I was the Mail-man" he replied, ignoring my questions. "I, and all the fairy-folk, have been and will always be, watching, guiding and protecting the magical bloodline that currently courses through your veins. For centuries now.. perhaps, even longer" he said.

"You have?? Why?" I said.

"Well, because, we take care of our own" he responded.

"I'm, I mean. We're like you…fairy people?" I asked.

"Of course, what did you think you were? And then, you chose to go to Earth, and we hand-picked the bloodline you would have and the experiences that would make you into you. Not an easy task by any measure, you must remember the greatest are those who suffer most, we call them ascended masters. One of the most valuable things in the entire universe, in all the universes, are lessons. The most valuable being the soul itself. The only way to really know a thing, is to experience it for yourself… You, my dear child, are an ascended master, an old soul.. Ascended means to climb or to rise, which one can only do by living many lives and learning lots of lessons. The journey on Earth is a lonely one —but what comes from it can only be described as beautiful, and all one must do to achieve it, is follow the signs of the path that has been mapped out for you" the Barefoot King said, passionately.

"So, you're expecting me to be grateful for bad times, shitty people, pain, loneliness and crippling grief?" I said. "Yes. You did say you were ready for the truth. Can you not see, there can be no good without evil, no light without dark, no courage without fear, no happiness without sadness, no life without death. Condemning the bad is but a pointless act, an idiocy, the only real thing to fear

—is yourself. You are your own worst enemy, the only force that can really stand in your way, the bad guys and the bad times are there to show you the strength and fortitude of your spirit, to show you what you can overcome using only the power of your soul. *What is a warrior without war?*" He said. "I duno — Rior?" I replied. "Very clever" he said, "but in a way, you are correct, a warrior without war is only a half of what they *could* be…"

The words of the barefoot king pulled me into a downward spiral. I hated when people said shit like: life is beautiful and abusive people should be thanked for creating a strong person, you should just move on and see life as the treasure it is, so you don't make other people feel uncomfortable that your life wasn't all sunshine and rainbows. It's a load of shit. *What if your life has been total crap?*

I'm supposed to neglect how I truly feel to make other people feel better about my hard times? Fuck that. Before I knew it, I was no longer standing with the Barefoot King. I was somewhere else. Somewhere dark.

Sucked into a black hole, a portal to an unknown destination.

Not in Kansas anymore. I'd left the fairy realm and fallen into the shadows.

It was cold, below temperatures conceivable to man, like nothing I've ever felt or experienced before. Cold to the bone. I was jackhammering uncontrollably. Everything in sight looked as if it had been burned and ash was floating in the brisk air.

The path was constructed from coal. Everything was grey and dull.

In the distance, I could vaguely see an old shack.

Out of thin air, a woman appeared.

"ARRRGHHH!" she screamed, full of rage directly in my face —
then she bolted away into a eery little house.

Her skin had a powdery, flakey appearance, as if she'd been
rolling around in murky talcum powder and papery ash for days
on end. Her eyes burnt into my very soul, glowing orange and red
with yellow flicks around her pupil, like a burning pit of fire. I
could feel so much pain, anger and pent up emotion emanating
through her eyes.

I felt as if I could recall every detail of her eyes, even though I had
only glanced at them for a brief tick of the clock. Her hair was
bright ginger and very long —all the way down her back.

She had come and gone in a flash.

While her florescent fiery eyes oozed my minds vision, and the
raw emotion I had witnessed lingered, I followed her into the
creepy little shack. If I had seen this on a scary movie, I'd be
saying, 'don't bloody go into the house you fool' as the
protagonist entered the building and came to their assured demise.
Alas, there I was inside a house with a young woman who
appeared to be some kind of demon creature.

Alone.

I came out of my thoughts, and began scanning the room looking
for the woman. The floor and walls were covered in the same grey
powder she was covered in. I found her cowering in fetal position
in the corner of the room, her face squished into the corner as if
she was trying to hide.

She was butt-naked, and crying profusely.

At the sight of her, I felt as if I was no longer in control of myself,
and before I could think twice about it, I was kneeling beside her,
my hand lying gently on her back in an attempt to comfort the

creepy naked lady collapsed crying on the floor. "Are you okay?" I said, softly.

I don't know why I felt so drawn to her. I sensed a connection to her —like I knew her very well. Like I had known her my whole life. I felt a familiarity between us. I had to help her, curiosity got the better of me (as usual) and I couldn't stop myself; this time it would surely, kill the cat.

The woman was making soft whimpering sounds, sobbing into her hands. Suddenly, as if she had levitated at lightning speed, we were standing, nose to nose, her chest puffed and eyes widened. Possessed.

"Do I fucking look okay to you? What, are you stupid or something? Fuckin' hell" she spat words out of her mouth like venom, almost hissing them. She had a snake like quality about her, her pupils were much like a cat or a snakes —little slits. Interestingly, I hadn't noticed the shape of her pupils before. Now that I could get a good look at her I realised she looked like an exact replica of me, only with different eyes, hair and weird flaky skin.

I don't recall how long I stood, frozen, staring into her fire-pit eyes, until I could string a few words together. "No..I..I..just.." I stuttered, I didn't have the faintest clue what to say to her now that I was here. I really hadn't thought this through well.

"You just what!??" a brief pause accompanied by a look to kill with eyes of pure villainy shooting through my spirit, my chest grew heavier and heavier as if rocks were piling higher and higher in my lungs. "I just want to help" I squeaked, looking down at the floor hoping to not catch her gaze. "You want to help?? Help how? How in the fuck would you be able to help me? With your poorly

constructed verbal communications, how will that help me? Do I look as if words could possibly save me? I live in hell. A secluded isle away from everybody…Why the fuck would you care anyway? They say I'm evil. A demon. *The witch.*
People don't associate with the evil-demon-witch type, let alone ask if they're okay. I've never heard such nonsense….Are you mad, girl?" The woman said, looking half ready to kill, half amused.

"Well I..I suppose, I care about the wellbeing of people, no matter who they are or what they are suspected of doing, or have done.." I said. "That's fucking stupid. In fact, it's up there with one of the stupidest things I've ever heard. Demons kill people you dumb bitch. Hmmm, actually, in saying that, I don't know why I haven't killed you yet" she said. "At a guess, it's because you can't. You're a parasite, if I'm not around what will you feed on?" I said, hoping my bluff would deter her. I had absolutely no idea if what I had just said was true, but I prayed it would buy me some time to figure out a way back to the Fairy Kingdom.

"How do you know it's not the other way around??..That you're the parasite and without me —the dark, the shadow, the shade, the bad and evil, there would be no light and you would quite literally cease to be"

I couldn't help but smile a little at her remark, in this moment I was incredibly grateful to what the barefoot king had shared with me.

"Ahh" I said with a tiny chuckle, "look at you, using your useless meaningless words to understand yourself and the others around you."

She was silent a moment then began blurting accusations at high speed, "how is all this 'caring' going for you? Hmm?" She said "Does anyone give a flying fuck about you? Do they notice anything you do for them?? Do they notice you at all? Who is there to pick you up when you fall?…. Let me guess..Ummm.. No-one. You're all alone and no-one gives a shit about you. Not one person would really care if you fell into the abyss, if you died and were never to be seen or heard from again. Hell, who knows, you might get a few fakers come to your pitiful funeral, like moths to a lamp trying to optimise their advantage and thrust it upon the people around them to gain some attention and sympathy, then before long, the rumours would emerge. They'd say you were mentally ill, that you died at your own hand, that there was always something wrong, something off about you, 'she just wasn't quite right' they'll all whisper about you. And you know what? Not one person would defend your name, your life or your honour. They don't care about you. I used to be like that, I cared and I wanted to help people. I used to be Nurse, I dedicated my life to caring for, and healing others but what good did it do? It didn't change how they treated me and it won't change for you. You're the weird girl, the odd kid that talks to trees, believes in magic and does weird shit all the time. Don't go near her, they say, she'll curse you. Ha! Your own family doesn't even love you. They say you're a liar, and tell others not to believe a word you say, we're normal they say —but Harlot doesn't even know up from down. The black sheep, hey?… And you think, pfft HA HA HA!" she interrupted herself with an intense bout of laughter. "You actually believe you can change your life, that in some way you are special and God has a plan for you?? Let me give you a little bit of advice. You can't change shit. God didn't help me when they tortured me for days and burnt me at a stake. Tell me, oh holy one, where was God then? Huh? The answer: nowhere, because God doesn't fuckin' exist" she said, staring at me with smug written across her face.

"…..Where are you from?" I asked.

The witch was sitting with knees bent leaning against the wall now, staring blankly into the floorboards, full of rage, yet, I could see only pain in her eyes. She looked up at me from the corner of her bright Autumn coloured eyes "a better question would be, *when*… I lived in Confinedville in 1645" she said and returned to where she was internally.

"Confinedville?" I repeated "so, were you really a witch then?… And you were burned for it?" I said.

"We were burned for being a witch, yes. For being being different to the rest of the flock of mindless sheep called society. For using herbs and plants to heal, for having opinions, for being sexually attractive and, of course, for being a woman" she said. "Wait. Hold up. What do you mean we? That doesn't make sense?" I questioned. A scandalous smirk manifested across her face, growing larger, masking a secret she wanted to reveal. Her expression had mischievous plastered across it as she snickered "Yes. Us. We. Me and you. You and I." She stated, calmly and much more collected than I really felt, I asked, "What do you mean by *us*?"

"Hmm..so I guess he hasn't told you everything? What I mean is what I said.

It's really quite simple my dear. Us. You and I, me and you. You and I.Same thing. Not a lot of difference, we are one and the same. I am you and you *were* me." She said.

I assumed someone so dark *must* be a manipulative liar, I denied her statement irrefutably. "I am nothing like you" I cried to her, unable to hold back my emotions, my tone was low and face expressionless but my voice broke with the weight of the truth as I spoke. An emotional outpour ran through me and I shouted at her, "who the hell are you, really?" I said.

"And what do you mean by that? Is it a question or a statement?…" she said. Her piercing eyes did nothing to me now that I was angry, my guard was up. "My name is Hazel Vermilliongate and I was the last witch burned to the stake during the Confinedville Witch Trials. I was accused of witchcraft by my dear old Ma and Pa. Lovely pair they were, I hope they're rotting in hell. Fucking assholes. No trial was held for me, because, why would parents condemn their own daughter. It couldn't possibly be out of spite. I used to get along with my Father when I was young, when he was buttering me up to become who they said I was supposed to be, but my Mother had other ideas, she would lose control of it all if I was High Priestess. She was never actually apart of it, but everyone knows she was in control of dear old Dad. Once we stop travelling and settled in Confinedtown, she turned everyone against me, she got my family to believe I would never fulfil my duties, she said I'd blow their cover and ruin their stupid little gang coven-y thingy and then she told the towns people I'd been doing witchcraft since I was a child and she couldn't stop me from hurting people. My cheating husband lit the flame. The flame that burned copiously around me bringing me slowly to my death. All due to the fact I was different, unique, for running to the beat of my own drum. For being powerful, the most fearful thing in the world to a flock is someone who can walk alone and simply be themselves. They slayed me in cold blood, without a second thought. My friends, my parents, my siblings and my lover watched mercilessly as a burned on a stake." She said. Hazel's eyes pained, her voice slightly heightening for second before moving ahead "Do you know what it's like when a human being is burnt alive??" she said, maliciously.

I wasn't sure if she actually wanted me to answer but I did just out of grace "ah, um, no… No I do not know what it is like when a human is burned alive, at all, and I suppose I have never really thought too much about it, I'm sorry, I'm really very sorry you had to go through that" I said. My speech was slow and unhinged, I think it took Hazel a little off guard. Empathy had always been one of my strong suits. My theory was that it came from all that reading, giving one the ability to put on someone else's shoes. Stories of hardship had always got to me, but this, Hazels horrific tale struck a cord in my heart, somewhere deep. I felt like I wanted to cry, but she wasn't crying so I held it back although my river of tears was becoming more and more difficult to hold in.

The pain was torture. Grief and misery plagued every aspect of my being, crushing my inner world like a giant wave pelting down on a stormy night in the middle of the ocean miles from land.

Hazel was glaring into space, an indescribable look of hurt scrolled across her face, her eyes swimming in fire, flames impishly swaying back and forth. She inhaled to speak. "The pain is excruciating, the brain and nervous system hit overload, the excessive amount of pain is unconceivable to the body and the internal organs. Death comes relatively quickly, even the grim reaper doesn't want to sit and watch someone burn. After the first inhale —you're gone. The soul ditches its host.

I couldn't completely leave my body so easily. I stayed to watch, I wanted to believe at least one person may weep as I burn. That just maybe, as I died, they'd regret the decision to take my life. I was sorely mistaken. Completely and utterly wrong.

The skin of my body melted in large sheets slowly dripped down my bones into the flames, blood and organs quick to follow, eaten up by the heat like meaningless plastic, much like the wrapper of a chocolate bar. By the time I had fully burned, no-one was left. Only me.

A lost soul, and a group of bones, praying for vengeance.

They left my bones at the sight of the burning and didn't bother to move, bury or pay any mind to my miserable death. They'd let all the bones of their victims pile up until they *had* to toss them out of the way to burn another witch. I was the last woman they burned alive so no-one ever returned to the spot I had died. The town I spent my childhood in, got married and hoped to start my own family in, a wish stolen from me without a second glance.. I was with child at the time of my burning. I named him Abel. We never met, but I just knew he was an Abel, like my brother..or should I say, nephew... a lost soul. Now he's a soul lost forever. My husband knew of my pregnancy. A fate too dull, too abrasive to wish upon your worst enemy. My husband had committed adultery, so it was convenient if I was dead, he could fuck everyone in town with no shame. An adulterer is simply a fool lacking self-control. A promiscuous widow receives sympathy. If he'd been caught he would have been squashed to death with boulders, so he let me burn and continued to do his thing guilt free. It took so many murders for the town to stop and see the stupidity. The sick thing is most of them knew it was wrong from the beginning, but after the first burning, they feared they'd gone too far to turn back so they kept going with their evil regime. Hundreds more were tortured and burned across the world after being accused and tried for witchcraft. Every 'witch' in Confinedville was killed in vain. First, they made our lives a living hell, then they threw us into the burning pit hell, leaving us to burn all alone." She said.

The room fell silent and a heaviness fell in the atmosphere. I could sense Hazels deep sorrow and defeat. An intense stabbing sensation crushing my chest as the blade of a grief stricken energetic knife cut away at me swiftly proceeding to jump into my throat and slash my insides. My eyes welled with tearful emotion as I contemplated what it must of been like to have experienced such an ordeal in real time, to have lived and re-lived that experience. Anger built on the inside, as rocks piled in my chest, rocks on fire, high temperature coals blazing. The burning inferno of fire combined with the stay power, and the stubbornness of the earth.

I tried to speak, to comfort her in some way but could only muster stuttered nonsense.

Hazel was right, words would fall short to comfort and heal on this occasion.

"What…What did you do to them?" I asked.

"Who? My family and the people who burned me? They got what they deserved. I'm a witch and witches curse people, so I made sure they'd burn for all eternity." She said.

"But, do you think that is the right thing to have done? What about forgiveness?" I asked.

"Fuck forgiveness. Action is the only thing that will help to move on. They say to treat people how you would like to be treated, so I simply gave them the treatment they asked for…not sure why you're all up on a high-horse, it's not like you have not cursed, even killed people in your time" she said.

"what?!? I most certainly have not" I replied.

"Oh, really? And what about that mirror shield you're always covering yourself in. It's a passive aggressive way to curse, but a curse none-the-less." She said.

"but…but I'm just trying to protect myself and throwing the energy back at them that they have thrown at me" I said.

"Haha, and what did I just say, love?"

I said nothing back. Silent in a pit of my own making. A deathly liquid of self-deprecating thoughts bombarding my head swirling around like a fine glass of red. I cleared my throat. "Oh, relax, we're all guilty. Whether it be by your own hand or claiming sovereignty and dominion over another's mind, sometimes doing something bad is good. If you don't defend yourself, you'll be eaten alive by those who seek out weakness and vulnerability because they feel like shit on the inside. We all know Witchcraft is a placebo —it only works if it's believes to work. A can curse only work if one believes themselves to be cursed" she said.

I leaned against the wall and slid all the way down to the floor, clutching at my knees. She continued to talk. "But, you know, that's what hurts the most, I was burned by people who were horrid, but believed they were good. For a long time I have believed I was bad, I believed them when they said there was something wrong with me. They tricked me into doubting myself."

I felt the weight of holding a grudge, carrying burdens and taking someone else's perception, and/or criticisms as fact. I could understand Hazel. I understood why she was so angry, how she had got here, and why she was *choosing* to live in her own personal hell. I could see the thought processes she must have gone through again and again with a fine-tooth comb. I realised she was punishing herself due to the actions of others, others that were misinformed, pigheaded and ignorant. She had punished herself much more than those that had hurt her. I decided not to make the same mistakes. Sometimes the best defence is to move on. I cannot change others and holding on to what they did won't change how they treated me. I deserve better.

Hazel began levitating in the middle of the room. Her fiery eyes had grown a blue ring on the outer edge of her iris. A bright gold light grew and beamed from every part of her.

I suppose talking about her pain had helped —it appeared she'd set herself free.

Hazel spirit flew across the room and collided with me, disappearing with a cloud of ash and dust.

And then, everything went black.

When I opened my eyes, I was in a haze of airborne dirt. I could hear gun shots in the distance. I sank lower into the trench I lay in. I couldn't see anything around me properly and the gun shots continued firing a few seconds longer, then slowed to roughly one shot per minute.

BANG!

I closed my eyes, screwing my face up closing my eyelids as tightly as possible.

Somewhere nearby a missile went off creating an abundance of debris in the air. As the smog began to fade, a man was revealed next to me —dressed head to toe in army attire, cameo-d up. Complete with a green bucket helmet and decked out with badges and medallions. An aura of pride surrounded him. He appeared to be no older than 19, his baby face unbroken.

"Get down Lass! Watch your head, these damn mongrels won't cease fire for a woman, no ruddy respect. Names Billy Lee Vermilliongate. Nice to finally meet ya —in the flesh, well, ah, in a sense anyhow…or, ahh, never-mind you get what I mean, aye" he said, extending his hand to shake mine.

"Am I supposed to know who you are?" I asked, as I politely shook his hand.

"Don't you recognise me from the photos?" He paused for a brief moment "well, that's a damn shame kiddo, I'm your great-great Grandfather and you're my great-great Granddaughter; I've been looking out for you since your birth, gets mighty hard in that land and I, along with a lot of others, have taken a special interest in you and your mission, need all the help you can conjure to pull all that off I'd reckon" he said. "I'm not sure what you mean, but, umm, thank you.. I guess… Can I ask why you're in this place all alone? Where are we? And what is going on here?" I said.

"I'm here on account o' the PTSD dear.. I think that's the terminology they use these days. When I got back form the war, I ain't never been the same since, it changed me to my core, left scars my soul… couldn't face the traumatic stress disorder when I was livin' so this is where I reside, re-living memories I'd buried deep in my subconscious, again and again. Every single day and every night. They don't tell you theres no escaping healin' while you're alive and now, I don't know anything but the pain, to be honest I think I kinda like it, it's safe, you know? I know what to expect. The familiarity of it…Gives me something to play out anyway, probably get bored otherwise" he said, gazing down at the dirt, sorrow locked behind his lime green eyes.

"How long have you been here, doing this?' I asked "why I'd say its been years and years now, over half a century at the very least" he said. "And where is your wife??..my great-great Grandmother?" I asked.

"Well I ain't seen or heard of her in many, many moons. I haven't a clue where she ended up. God…I haven't even thought of her since I've been here. I guess my depression got the better of me. Makes ya selfish, ya see. I'm consumed, slowly being eaten away in a shallow cloud of maddening repetition. That's why you Harls, are the answer. Complete your mission and set me free.

Set us all free. It's time for our bloodline to change. Drug and alcohol addiction, abusive parenting styles, mental illnesses, the slandering and betrayal. Break the pattern. The blood in your veins doesn't control you. You don't have to be like them, like me. It doesn't need to run in the family anymore. Choose your own door, for yourself. Wake up, it's time now" he said, pushing me into a pool of thought causing me to experience a feeling of falling, descending lower and lower.

Until my body roughly jerked awake.

I was lying down on a wooden floor. Black sails with a skull and bones, gusting in the wind.

I stood up and looked around. I was now on a big wooden ship, hair blowing in the powerful wind. The shore seemed miles and miles away, ocean as far as the eye could see.

I had no clue where I was, who I would meet or how to get back and finish my conversation with the Barefoot King —and it was just getting good, then somehow, for whatever reason I got lost again, in this odd, peculiar, very weird place. A stranger in a strange land. "Well, hello there stranger!" A woman's voice cried out "I've been waiting for you, so long I thought I'd almost go quite mad, I've got so many things to tell you. I can't believe it, finally, a modern day prophet here with me on my ship! I was once like you, ready to go, an idea, a dream, to make it all happen, I did what they all said I couldn't, defied the odds and did it my way, but I will say, to follow ones heart isn't all they say. The back lash is wicked, the push back fierce, ain't no rest for the wicked, if you want to do what has never been done" she said.

I wanted to listen to her talk all day. Here voice was husky and alluring. She spoke the way *Amy Winehouse* sings. "They hate and they gossip" she continued "throwing banana peels in your way, hoping you'll fall, flat on your face. The journey is long, but oh, so rewarding, and I'm counting on you so I too, can live on. My spirit is rebellious, I need a good cause to get behind, to use my precious energy for, so I can feel alive again." The strange lady came closer to me as she spoke, she was a classic beauty, the type of looks that are pleasing to everyone. She was the kind of person that would stand out in a crowd without even trying. Her sandy coloured hair flowing with the wind, the sun catching flickers of natural blonde highlights with eyes of lilac, calming like lavender. "Do I know you?" I asked.

"Why, of course! I'm the you buried deep, deep down, the one you don't let yourself be. A spiritual cousin you could say. Oh! You must remember me, I've followed you around for yonks, I used to visit and we'd chat for hours and hours, remember? In the days you lived up the trees, climbing and playing around. I'd sail to the tree tops and you'd giggle at me with the innocence only a child can possess, my ship sailing on thin air higher than the tree top" she said rhythmically, as if at any moment she might burst into song. Her proud personality boasting confidence and showiness. I wanted to give her all my attention, everything about her made me want to stare at her for days, her smile and her body, the unusual style only she could pull off —if *Jack Sparrow* met V*ogue*. Although something about her, despite how drawn to her I felt, made me want to stay away from her, as if I had to keep my distance for my own safety. I already wanted to please her and do whatever she said.

She was the most striking, well-mannered and well-spoken individual I'd come into contact with today. It wasn't even that she said everything was correct or punctual but that she did her very own thing with confidence. Some of the larger words she said I was sure she'd made up and her manner wasn't common, yet, her mannerisms made me want to love her, to take care of her, to believe whatever she said. A beautiful liar.

"Can I ask for your name? I'm sorry I don't remember the days I climbed trees, I've pushed all that away. It almost feels like another life, I sometimes question if that was really even me… A girl without worries enjoying the simplicity of the trees" I said.

"Hmmmphhh" she growled and threw her arms to her side much like a child would.

"You will get it soon, there's no way you could not. Nothing is ever lost, we only fail to see, it's still there in our heads, volted away, complied in files titled, forget to keep me sane….Anyway my name is Tillie, but you can call me Tee, that's what they all call me, my crew that is" she said.

"Your crew? Where are they? And what are you doing on this ship?" I said. After the stories I'd heard so far on this wacky adventure I was on, I knew better than to expect anything based on appearance or first impressions.

"Well, I guess you could say I'm a pirate, a Robin Hood of the sea, taking from the rich and giving to the poor.. the poor, including me" she said.

"So..you steal from people?" I said.

"I would call it bringing balance to the world, I seek an equilibrium of society. Where all are equal, no matter the cost or what is in their pockets. We all have needs, material satiety is so small, the real needs are spiritual, and that I want to see, for material counts for nil on this side of the veil, 'cause golly, by then you recognise the meaning of it all, is to learn and to experience, and revolutionise the soul" she said.

"Okay, sure… And what about the where about of your crew?" I said.

"*Our* crew. You know them well. Every bad thought or unpleasant impulse you've ever had..but they're gone now, every single one of them, pushed down too far so they quit. Our mission is much too hefty a feat, not for the weak, so they jumped ship" she said. "I am so sick of hearing about a bloody mission. What's the fucking mission?" I said. She gave me a look to say I was stupid.

"To *live*." She said.

"And how do you suppose I know your crew? I think you're quite mad." I said.

"Goodness gracious you are thick. Where the hell do you think you are right now?" she said. "Could be hell" I said.
"Hell isn't real, not in the way you think anyway. Hell is your guilt and your shame — guilt and shame can be an all consuming foe, one can run and hide form it in intervals while on the physical plane, but it doesn't work like that here. It's all consuming, an endless maze, a unsolvable puzzle, where a piece is missing. A part of the soul sold and stolen. A feat, is an achievement that requires great courage, and courage means to possess a heart. You do not accept all of yourself, so you are an empty half-person." she said. "What would you feel guilty from?" I asked.
"I do not feel any guilt, but you do *for* me. In legal terminology my crew and I are the murderers, the kidnappers, the thieves, the capturers, the violet, the damned and the broken. Sick people with no empathy for others. In my era, they called us pirates, but you know, these are all just words and labels, meaningless really… Nothing compares to or describes the feeling of the act, and the thrill of the escape to the open sea much like the victim, never to be seen or heard from again" she said. As she spoke she looked down, rarely glimpsing up and dropping the gaze every time I met her eyes. Right away my inner dialogue told me to bail, and go anywhere but here, with someone like her.
There was no way I could understand her or her actions and the villainy of the path she had chosen to take. At this point I asked myself, what is the worst that could happen? I don't think I can die here, and even if she could kill me, I'd rather die than stay here on this ship wth her. At least I'd get a good story out of her.
I cleared my throat to speak "What is it that you've done?" I said.
She stared at me, then smiled widely. "I would love to tell you"

she said, and for the first time since I'd met Tillie, she looked directly into my eyes. "Interesting, isn't it? Evil is always disguised. Beauty is alluring and can be used a weapon, just as the lack thereof can help one to fly under the radar, and used as the advantage. We must use what we have to our advantage. Unsuspecting and trusting victims get a feeling of safety and comfort when looking into pretty eyes. You must master the art of spirit filled eyes, to replicate the appearance of soul through the looking glasses. I can teach you to create that feeling of home. Let me take control. Aren't you tired of being the victim? I will show you how to be the predator —instead of the prey. Welcome to my Wonderland." She said and then Tillie lifted her boney pale hand and placed it on my shoulder.

In a split second she'd created a portal and we were transported through her eyes.. to the inside of a beautiful monster. Inside her mind, was complete and utter turmoil. Chaos and mayhem. Screeching cries of past victims playing on repeat. Blood poured from the sky as thick red rain. The stench in the air was less than desirable, the earth we stood upon was moist and decaying. There was static in the atmosphere. The feeling of death and horror. Broken pieces of wood burned slowly, scattered randomly around her bleak scene of misery and betrayal. I turned my head to study Tillie's facial expression. I was always curious what made people like her tick. I longed to know how she came to be so disturbed and distorted. Tillie was basking in the ambience of her sick state of mind. She lifted her head, opened her mouth and enjoyed the red rain as if she hadn't experienced the feeling of wet for years. She bathed in the blood, smiling and rubbing her hands over her face, stretched her arms out to spin in a circle while chuckling like an amused happy child.

Thud!

A little girl bumped into my thigh, and quickly ran off, whimpering. Another version of Tillie followed closely behind her. She chased the young girl behind a burnt abandoned ship on the sandy blood stained beach. Screaming and profanities could be heard from behind the ship. A sudden splat of blood showed itself at the side of the ship, then a blood covered Tillie emerged, grinning, ear to ear. Pleased with herself and what she had done. I rushed around to the other side of the boat to save the little girl. When I got to her she was covered in her own blood. Tears dripped from my face. Tillie took a step back. I reached down to turn the face down little girl over, she would have been only eight years old. Gasping for air I couldn't believe my eyes. The little girl was me. I suddenly realised I was holding a knife. I dropped it and kneeled to the terrified and bleeding younger version of me, hugging her and repeatedly saying 'I'm sorry' until the moment she took a large inhale —and died.

Scene after scene, different versions of me, at different ages and stages of life came out of thin air, running, chased by a crazed Tillie, the hunt poisoning her eyes making them pure black. She slaughtered every one of them, without any hesitation or second thought. A total lack of compassion or empathy. Hearing not one plea for mercy. Vomit crawled into my throat.

I noticed her smile grew smaller and smaller with each kill she committed, dissatisfaction written across her face. "The problem is" the Tillie standing next to me said, "the high of the kill never last. You are always stuck trying to relive it, to feel the high of the first time, but it is never and will never be like the first. It grows emptier and emptier, like an addiction to drugs, the feeling lessens as your tolerance grows." She said casually. My face screwed up in confusion, eyes wide and unblinking.

It took some time to talk.

"They're not all really here, are they? Playing out their last moments again and again, with you and that crazed look in your eye?!? Tell me they're not!" I said.

Tillie looked at me wickedly "they are… in a sense anyway, I took a piece of their soul when I stole their life, and they a part of mine.. pretty cool, huh? It comforts me to know that after all these years I will still be in their thoughts. I am led to question; who wants their story told the most? The victim" —she pronounced victim with sarcasm in her tone, as if it wasn't a real thing and none of these people had really suffered at her hands "or the perpetrator, AKA, me" she said with a foul, stomach curling giggle.

"So.." she said "whacha think?..Describe it to me..don't leave out the details, please."

I shook my head in disbelief. Her words and way of thinking, her actions, made me feel physically sick, in a non-physical land.

Did this bitch just actually laugh about what she'd done?

"What the fuck is wrong with you??!!?" I screamed, only inches from her face.

As I said these words to Tillie, a look of shock came to her face, eyes full of wonderment. If only, for a split second —then all sign of emotion left. She stood up straight, correcting her posture and puffing her chest out, pulling her jacket together, her hands meeting in the middle.

Then just like that, the scenery changed. We were back on the ship, sailing on the beautiful vast open water. "Nothing" She muttered, looking to the floor of her ship.

"Nothing is wrong with me" she said.

I had nothing to say to her, I wanted nothing to do with her.

"You killed her! It was you! What's the difference between you and I? You are just like me! You've been killing versions of yourself for years, never allowing yourself to just be you, chopping your head off for the sake of others. You've lost touch with who you once were when you were a little girl, running from who you truly are and masquerading as someone else, time and time again, to be who you think people think you should be. You're weak and worthless, you'll never make it through. I own you and I'll keep telling you what to do." Tillie said.

As she spoke, her lizard appearance showed, her true identity shining through, scales and thin lips with sharp pupils that could cut through steal. Ugly.

She grew larger and larger, turned green, and her tongue split down the middle.

I froze on the inside. "I am not like you" I said, firmly, trying to mask the fear I felt; and I punched her in the mouth.

"How's that for heart?" I said.

With that, she rushed at me full speed with mouth full of blood, spear tackling me into the depths of the ocean.

Once I hit water, Tillie vanished, leaving me all alone, sinking into an unknown abyss as if I was being dragged down by a ball and chain attached to my ankle.

I was still able to breath under water —yet it was no less terrifying. The water surrounding me grew colder and colder, darker and darker. Soon it was pitch black.

The fear of what creatures may lurk beneath the sea surface consumed my mind. I was in pain from the sub-zero temperature. The day thus far a distant memory. Sinking further and further, descending into the unknown dark territory.

Terror left and a depression began to sink in as if a process of osmosis was occurring from the dark cold water. First, I had a feeling of despair then, nothingness. I stopped caring if I would survive or if I'd die. All I wanted was to do was stop falling, to feel something else —anything at all. It may have been hours or days, weeks, possibly even a month of sinking into total darkness. Alone.

At this point I longed for Tillie's return, any company would do. As the loneliness crept in, I began to feel something sticking to me, covering the whole left side of my body. It was sticky and scaly and felt disgusting. I panicked and turned to push it off with my right hand, but this only made it stick to me even more, clinging with all its might. I wiggled and struggled with everything I had, trying to break free as I moved its grip grew tighter, like a Chinese finger trap. It was beginning to suffocate me.

"Ahh!" I cried out in an exhausted frustration. "Get the fuck off me!!" I began sobbing in angst, the silence around me getting louder and louder.

"Oh! Harlot, please don't be like that! We're meant to be together, forever and always" said a voice, breaking the silence. I couldn't see anything so I felt around to examine the creature that was now glued to me. I touched two heads, and goopy goo, it was hard to move my hand once I touched its icky body.

"Who are you? I cannot see anything" I said, my hands stuck on each head. I think by this stage, my surprise gauge had expired.

"The love of your life, of course, silly Harlot" one head said, "no I am!" The other whined. "I need you Harlot, I could never survive without you, please stay with me, or I don't know what I'd do, I'd surely die!" The first head said. One of the voices tone was whiney, the other demanding and condescending. My drop into the unknown somehow slowed with the slimy creature attached to me, I started to feel as if I was going backwards.

"Um, I'm sorry, I don't know you guys" I said.

"Don't know us?!?" they yelled in unison. To this day, it's still the creepiest thing I've ever heard. "How could you say that? We've been with you your whole life through, here deep in the shadows, ready and willing to protect you whenever you needed us! Harlot! Please! Take that back, say it isn't so! We've always been there for you, we were there when everyone else left, when you were alone, cold and crying on the floor, we were there! You know us, my name is Co, and that's Dependancy!" The whiney head said.

Eyes widening I pieced together the intricate puzzle of where I was, who all these beings were and what was going on. The heads continued speaking to each other.

"Maybe we should leave her too" the angry head said, "she doesn't even know us, or remember everything we're done for her the bloody little ingrate! Ya think know someone! But no, take take take and give nothing in return. Fuck her, let's leave the bitch to die here and rot alone!"

"We cant! She needs us! Only we can help her! I love her, and she loves us! I'm sure of it. How could she not!?! No we cant leave, we made a deal and now we are with her for life" the whiney head said. "She doesn't give a fuck about us!" The angry head snapped, "who cares, she's worthless and we will be better off."

I sat listening to the pair of heads bicker between one another. Contemplating what was going on. A peculiar familiarity kicked in. I think I did know them.

I had known them for a very long time.

I had confided in them, used them in my relationships…helped to create them.

It was then I could see a tiny glimmer in the darkness.

A flicker of golden warm flame appeared before me, and the creature squealed then disappeared all at once. Light emanated around me in a bright white-golden sparkles.

I was completely calm in this moment —then as quickly as it had appeared, it was gone.

Everything happens so quickly here, and no-one sticks around for long.

With the blink of my eyes, I was finally back with the Barefoot King.

"..What is a warrior without war?" He said, and handed me a book. The book I had ditched days ago. The book of my past and future. I opened the book, and it was blank.

The king smiled. "And that's that. You're free to choose your own life. I bid you farewell, brave-soul" the King said, as he walked slowly and directing me to the door. I extended my arm to reach for the door handle, pulling the door open to reveal the where I came from.

"Wait! You never told me why you aren't wearing any shoes?"

"Simple" he said with the cheeky smile he wore as an accessory, and then, just like that he disappeared too.

'Well, Barefoot King, you're really missing out on the power of a good pair of shoes. So long, my friend..' I said to myself quietly, and waved goodbye to the other world.

I opened my eyes and I was back where it all began, staring at the once unimpressive, now beautiful tree. From the corner of my eye I could see a figure, I turned my head and there she was again. The beautiful blonde-haired blue-eyed woman with the red dress.

"Hello" I said.

"Welcome back, my love, it is very nice to speak with you, finally! I have been watching and waiting from afar, for you to be ready for me, for you to accept and discover who you truly are" she said.

"...And who are you? May I ask?"

" I am a woman who made a mistake and took my own life, leaving my life behind" she said. "I feel like I already know you.." I said.

"You could say we know each other very well, I am a potential life path of yours. You could be me, or you could not. I hope that you won't be, I love you very much and I wish for you to be all you can be, for you to live. There has to be another way" she said.

A rainbow appeared behind her, and she floated away into the clouds.

I will take this second chance.

A diagnosis does not define me. I am not crazy, I am special. I can see things others cannot. I was off with the fairies, met a past life, an ancestor and the darkest parts of myself; discovered who I truly am, gained a fresh perspective—and survived. I have the ability to be one person one day, another the next, someone else in an hour and then another.

I am glad to be me and I am ready to live.

****

Perspective switch
2.0

****

The Asylum

Dull and gloomy.

Dr. Hodoyafel sat across from Harlot holding the pages Harlot had written. "Harlot, do you remember what happened the night you tried to commit suicide?" Dr. Hodoyafel asked. "Yes" Harlot said. Dr. Hodoyafel asked Harlot if her recollection of what had happened was what she had written in the pages she held. "Yes" Harlot said.

"Harlot, this is not what happened. You got a knife, cut you wrists and you almost died. Since then, you have been here, in this room at the asylum — all of this is delusion" said Dr. Hodoyafel. "You fucking lying cunt!! I know that you're working for them! I know that's why you keep saying I'm crazy!! You're trying to keep me locked up and keep their secret safe! Let me out of here you fucking bitch!" Harlot screamed, strapped to the bed she lye on, unable to move too much but she was thrashing her body around as much as she could. She really wasn't helping her plea to sanity.

This was not the first time Harlot had become enraged, or violent — in the asylum, or on the outside. Once, she had head-butted a 6 foot 4 grown ass man, because he asked her to go back to her room. She had to be injected with sedatives to calm her down. There were a few other incidents and altercations —if someone said something Harlot didn't like, or didn't want to do, it was possible that she may turn on them. It was quite strange, she only behaved this way on certain days, in certain moods —with certain eyes. Harlot assaulted Dr. Hodoyafel the first time she'd told Harlot she was experiencing delusions and that she believed Harlot may suffer with Schizophrenia.

"Harlot, what you have written confirms the ill state of mind you are in. This is insanity. You have been in this room for weeks. You did not go to another land and you have spoken with no-one but me." Dr. Hodoyafel said.

"Really?" Harlot's eyes turned slightly lilac, and she raised an eyebrow, "if you don't let me out of here now, I'll kill you first you stupid cunt" she said, calmly.

Dr. Hodoyafel got up to leave the room, she turned locking the bright-red door behind her with the ring she was wearing, and went on to treat her next patient.

If you or someone you know is struggling with mental health issues, please seek a mental health professional.